Wilson County Fair

Award-Winning Recipes

Wilson County Promotions, Inc.

Wilson County Fair

Award-Winning Recipes

Published by Wilson County Promotions, Inc.

P.O. Box 1203
Lebanon, Tennessee 37088
615-443-2626
This cookbook is a collection of favorite recipes,
which are not necessarily original recipes.

ISBN:0-9774444-0-6
Edited, Designed, and Manufactured by
Community Classics

CommunityClassics™

An imprint of

FRP™

P.O. Box 305142
Nashville, Tennessee 37230
800-358-0560

Photographers:
Peggy Clemons
Perry Harmon
T.A. Roberson
Rick Thorne

Manufactured in China
First Printing: 2006
4,000 copies

Baking Committee

Debbie Stephens, *Chairman*

Lynda Ann Sparkman, *Co-Chair*

Ray Lynn Crutcher

Kathy Haskins

Linda Neal

Dora Lynn Sparkman

Kelly Wright

Table of Contents

Historical Time Line of the Wilson County Fair

1853-1885: The Third Division Fair was held in Lebanon. This fair was originally located on Coles Ferry Pike, the site of today's Jimmy Floyd Center and Lebanon's Senior Citizens Center.
1919: The first fair of the 20th century was held for two days in the courthouse on the square in Lebanon.
1920: Homer Hancock, Tennessee's Commissioner of Agriculture, was the first president of the Tennessee Association of Fairs.
1920–1927: A Fair Board was organized, stock was sold, and twenty acres was purchased near the old "fair spring" on Coles Ferry Pike. $30,000 in improvements were made, including a grandstand, stable, and cattle barn. These were followed with a poultry building and women's building. In 1927, Fair attendance was 25,000.
1927–1969: The Wilson County Fair had various owners and stockholders and continued at various intervals until it closed in 1969 as a stockholder fair.
1973–1978: The Lebanon Jaycees reestablished a fair in Wilson County called the Midstate Fair.
1974: The James E. Ward Agriculture Center and Community Center was established with the purchase of 104 acres by the Wilson County Commission.
1979: Wilson County Promotions was chartered with the purpose of establishing The Wilson County Fair. Thirty-three members were on the first Fair Board with twenty-one members on the Youth Board. Attendance was 12,000.

1984: Tennesse's Most Improved Fair. Fifty-six members were on the Fair Board. Attendance was 21,000.
1988: Hale Moss, President of the Wilson County Fair, was elected as President of the Tennessee Association of Fairs.
1990: Ground breaking for Fiddler's Grove
1991: State Champion Fair of AAA Division
1992: Tennessee's Champion of Champion Fairs
1993: Tennessee's Champion of Champion Fairs for a second time
1999: Tennssee's State Champion Fair. Andy Brummett is elected as President of the Tennessee Association of Fairs. Attendance tops 257,000.
2000: Wilson County Fair is named Champion of Champions with an attendance of 280,000. The James E. Ward Agricultural Center has grown from 104 acres to 244 acres.
2001: Attendance tops 311,000. James Spears is elected to Tennessee Association of Fairs Board of Directors.
2002: Wilson County Fair nabbed the title of Tennessee's newly created category Triple A Champion Fair in Tennessee. Attendance is 328,300, with a volunteer Fair Board of 300 volunteers.
2003: Attendance soars to more than 360,000.
2004: Wilson County Fair is voted Tennessee's Premier Fair.
2005: Attendance is 411,068. The Fair theme is "Bright Lights and Summer Nights." Fiddler's Grove includes forty-seven buildings.

Dedication

To all the participants in the 2004-2005

Wilson County Fair baking contests

who have willingly shared

their talents and recipes.

This cookbook ensures the continuation

of this tradition at Wilson County Fairs

for future generations.

Cakes

Angel Cake

1 1/2 cups sifted confectioners' sugar
1 cup sifted cake flour or sifted all-purpose flour
1 1/2 cups egg whites (11 or 12 eggs)
1 1/2 teaspoons cream of tartar
1 teaspoon vanilla extract
1/2 teaspoon salt
1 cup granulated sugar

Sift the confectioners' sugar and flour together. Sift the mixture 2 additional times. Beat the egg whites, cream of tartar, vanilla and salt at medium speed in a mixing bowl until soft peaks form. Add the granulated sugar, 2 tablespoons at a time, beating constantly until stiff peaks form. Fold in half the flour mixture. Fold in the remaining flour mixture, 1/4 at a time. Spoon the mixture into an ungreased tube pan. Bake at 350 degrees for 50 minutes or until the top is brown and dry. Invert onto a funnel to cool completely. Loosen the cake from the side of the pan. Invert onto a cake plate.

Petra Mitchell, Watertown

Angel Food Cake

1 1/2 cups sifted cake flour
12 egg whites
1 1/4 teaspoons cream of tartar
1/4 teaspoon salt
1/4 teaspoon vanilla extract
1/4 teaspoon almond extract
1 1/3 cups sugar

Sift the flour 4 times into a bowl. Beat the egg whites, cream of tartar, salt, vanilla and almond extract at high speed in a mixing bowl for 5 minutes or until stiff peaks form. Add the sugar, 1/3 cup at a time, beating well after each addition. Fold in the flour. Pour into an ungreased 10-inch tube pan. Bake at 375 degrees for 35 minutes. Invert the pan onto a wire rack and let stand for 1 hour or until the cake is completely cool. Loosen the cake from the side of the pan. Invert onto a cake plate.

Amy Upchurch, Watertown

Angel Food Loaf

1/2 cup sifted cake flour
1/2 cup sugar
2/3 cup egg whites (5 or 6 eggs), at room temperature
1/8 teaspoon salt
1/2 teaspoon cream of tartar
1/4 cup sugar
1/2 teaspoon vanilla extract

Sift the flour and 1/2 cup sugar together 4 times. Beat the egg whites and salt in a mixing bowl until foamy. Add the cream of tartar and beat until soft peaks form. Add 1/4 cup sugar, 2 tablespoons at a time, beating constantly until blended. Beat in the vanilla. Sift half the flour mixture over the egg mixture. Fold in lightly. Fold in the remaining flour mixture. Pour into an ungreased 5×10-inch loaf pan. Bake at 375 degrees for 25 minutes. Invert the pan onto a wire rack. Let stand for 1 hour or until the cake is completely cool before removing from the pan.

Corky Sharpe, Mt. Juliet

Fresh Apple Cake

CAKE
2 cups sugar
$1^1/_2$ cups vegetable oil
3 eggs, beaten
3 cups all-purpose flour
1 teaspoon salt
1 teaspoon baking soda
2 teaspoons vanilla extract
3 cups chopped apples
1 cup chopped pecans

BROWN SUGAR TOPPING
$^1/_3$ cup margarine
$^1/_4$ cup evaporated milk
1 cup packed brown sugar
1 teaspoon vanilla extract

For the cake, combine the sugar, oil and eggs in a mixing bowl and mix well. Sift the flour, salt and baking soda together. Add the dry ingredients to the egg mixture and mix well. Stir in the vanilla, apples and pecans. The batter will be stiff. Pour into a greased tube pan. Bake at 350 degrees for $1^1/_4$ hours.

For the topping, heat the margarine, evaporated milk and brown sugar in a saucepan until the margarine is melted, stirring frequently. Bring to a boil and boil for 3 minutes, stirring constantly. Remove from the heat and stir in the vanilla. Spread over the warm cake.

Sherry Carr, Lebanon

Cinnamon Apple Cake

CAKE

2 cups sifted cake flour
2 cups sugar
2 teaspoons ground cinnamon
1 teaspoon baking soda
1/4 teaspoon salt
2 eggs
1 cup vegetable oil
1 teaspoon vanilla extract
4 cups chopped apples
1/2 cup chopped pecans

VANILLA GLAZE

1 cup packed light brown sugar
1/2 cup (1 stick) margarine
1/4 cup milk
1 teaspoon vanilla extract

For the cake, sift the flour, sugar, cinnamon, baking soda and salt together. Beat the eggs and oil in a mixing bowl until light and foamy. Add the vanilla and mix well. Add the dry ingredients and beat until blended. Stir in the apples and pecans. Pour into a greased 9×13-inch cake pan. Bake at 350 degrees for 1 hour.

For the glaze, heat the brown sugar, margarine and milk in a saucepan. Bring to a boil and boil for 2 1/2 minutes, stirring constantly. Remove from the heat and stir in the vanilla. Pour over the warm cake.

Corky Sharpe, Mt. Juliet

Apple Cake with Brown Sugar Glaze

CAKE

2 cups sugar
1 1/2 cups vegetable oil
2 eggs
2 teaspoons vanilla extract
2 1/2 cups self-rising flour
3 cups shredded apples
1 cup chopped pecans

BROWN SUGAR GLAZE

1/4 cup (1/2 stick) butter
1/2 cup packed brown sugar
1/3 cup milk

For the cake, beat the sugar, oil and eggs in a bowl until light and fluffy. Stir in the vanilla. Add the flour gradually, mixing constantly. Fold in the apples and pecans. Pour into a bundt pan. Bake at 350 degrees for 55 to 60 minutes or until the cake tests done. Let cool in the pan for 15 minutes. Invert onto a cake plate.

For the glaze, combine the butter, brown sugar and milk in a saucepan and bring to a boil. Boil for 3 minutes, stirring constantly. Pour over the warm cake.

Nancy Harp, Lebanon

Apple Cake with Cream Cheese Frosting

CAKE
$1^3/4$ cups sugar
1 cup vegetable oil
2 eggs
$2^1/2$ cups self-rising flour
1 teaspoon ground cinnamon
1 teaspoon vanilla extract
1 (21-ounce) can apple pie filling, apples chopped
1 cup chopped pecans

CREAM CHEESE FROSTING
8 ounces cream cheese, softened
$^1/2$ cup (1 stick) margarine, softened
2 teaspoons vanilla extract
2 cups confectioners' sugar

For the cake, beat the sugar, oil and eggs in a mixing bowl until light and fluffy. Add the flour, cinnamon and vanilla and beat for 2 to 3 minutes or until blended. Stir in the pie filling and pecans. Pour into a bundt pan or tube pan. Bake at 300 degrees for $1^1/4$ hours or until a wooden pick inserted in the center comes out clean. Cool in the pan.

For the frosting, combine the cream cheese and margarine in a mixing bowl and beat until creamy. Add the vanilla and mix well. Add the confectioners' sugar and beat until the mixture is blended and of a spreading consistency. Spread over the cooled cake.

Betty Weatherby, Lebanon

Spiced Apple Cake

CAKE

3 cups unbleached all-purpose flour
2 teaspoons ground cinnamon
1/2 teaspoon nutmeg
1 teaspoon baking soda
1/2 teaspoon salt
1 cup packed light brown sugar
1 cup granulated sugar
1 1/2 cups vegetable oil
3 eggs
2 1/2 teaspoons vanilla extract
5 apples, peeled and chopped
1 1/2 cups chopped pecans

SUGAR GLAZE

1/4 cup (1/2 stick) unsalted butter
1/4 cup packed light brown sugar
1/4 cup granulated sugar
Pinch of salt
1/2 cup heavy cream or whipping cream

For the cake, sift the flour, cinnamon, nutmeg, baking soda and salt together. Cream the brown sugar, granulated sugar and oil in a mixing bowl until light and fluffy. Add the eggs 1 at a time, beating well after each addition. Add the flour mixture gradually, beating constantly. Stir in the vanilla, apples and pecans. Spoon the mixture into a buttered and floured 9×13-inch cake pan. Bake at 325 degrees for 1 1/4 hours or until a wooden pick inserted in the center comes out clean. Cool in the pan.

For the glaze, melt the butter in a saucepan. Add the brown sugar, granulated sugar and salt and cook over medium-low heat for 2 minutes. Stir in the cream and bring the mixture to a boil. Boil for 2 minutes, stirring constantly. Remove from the heat. Poke holes in the cake with a wooden pick. Pour the warm glaze over the cake.

Susan Wright, Mt. Juliet

Applesauce Cake with Caramel Frosting

CAKE

2 1/2 cups all-purpose flour
1 1/2 cups sugar
1 teaspoon baking powder
1/2 teaspoon salt
1 1/2 teaspoons ground cinnamon
1/2 teaspoon nutmeg
1 1/2 cups applesauce
1/2 cup (1 stick) butter or margarine, melted
2 eggs
1 teaspoon vanilla extract
1 cup chopped peeled apple
1/2 cup chopped walnuts

CARAMEL FROSTING

1 cup packed brown sugar
1/2 cup (1 stick) butter or margarine
2 tablespoons evaporated milk
1/2 teaspoon salt
Sifted confectioners' sugar

For the cake, combine the flour, sugar, baking powder, salt, cinnamon and nutmeg in a bowl and mix well. Add the applesauce, butter, eggs and vanilla and beat for 2 minutes or until blended. Stir in the apple and walnuts. Pour into a greased and floured 9×13-inch cake pan. Bake at 350 degrees for 35 to 40 minutes or until a wooden pick inserted in the center comes out clean.

For the frosting, combine the brown sugar, butter, evaporated milk and salt in a saucepan. Cook over low heat until the butter is melted and the brown sugar is dissolved, stirring frequently. Remove from the heat and let stand until cool. Stir in enough confectioners' sugar to reach the desired spreading consistency. Spread over the cooled cake.

Margaret Thompson Kilgore, Lebanon

Applesauce Raisin Cake

CAKE

1/2 cup (1 stick) butter, softened
1 cup sugar
1 egg, beaten
1 1/2 cups applesauce
2 cups all-purpose flour
2 teaspoons baking cocoa
1 teaspoon ground cinnamon
1/2 teaspoon nutmeg
1/8 teaspoon salt
3/4 cup raisins
3/4 cup chopped pecans
1/4 cup hot water
2 teaspoons baking soda
1 teaspoon vanilla extract

BUTTERY BROWN SUGAR GLAZE

1/2 cup packed brown sugar
1/4 cup milk
1/2 cup (1 stick) butter

For the cake, cream the butter and sugar in a mixing bowl until light and fluffy. Add the egg and applesauce and mix well. Sift the flour, baking cocoa, cinnamon, nutmeg and salt together. Add the raisins and pecans and toss to coat. Add to the applesauce mixture gradually, beating constantly. Combine the water and baking soda in a small bowl and mix well. Stir into the applesauce mixture. Stir in the vanilla. Pour into 2 greased and floured 9-inch round cake pans. Bake at 350 degrees for 35 minutes. Cool in the pan for 10 minutes. Remove to a wire rack to cool completely.

For the glaze, combine the brown sugar, milk and butter in a heavy saucepan. Bring to a boil. Boil for 2 minutes, stirring constantly. Remove from the heat and let cool until lukewarm. Spread between the layers and over the top and side of the cake.

Corky Sharpe, Mt. Juliet

Applesauce Cake with Apple Glaze

CAKE

2 cups cake flour, sifted
2 teaspoons pumpkin pie spice
1 cup granulated sugar
1/2 cup packed brown sugar
1 cup (2 sticks) butter, softened
3 eggs
2 cups hot applesauce
2 teaspoons baking soda
1/2 cup raisins
1/2 cup chopped pecans, almonds or walnuts

APPLE GLAZE

1/2 cup packed brown sugar
1/2 cup granulated sugar
6 tablespoons butter
1/2 cup apple juice
1/4 cup milk
1 1/2 teaspoons vanilla extract

For the cake, combine the flour and pumpkin pie spice in a bowl. Cream the granulated sugar, brown sugar and butter in a mixing bowl until light and fluffy. Add the eggs 1 at a time, beating well after addition. Combine the applesauce and baking soda in a small bowl and mix well. Add to the creamed mixture and beat until blended. Add the flour mixture and mix well. Stir in the raisins and pecans. Pour the mixture into a greased and floured tube pan. Bake at 350 degrees for 50 minutes. Cool in the pan for 15 minutes. Invert onto a serving plate.

For the glaze, combine the brown sugar, granulated sugar, butter, apple juice, milk and vanilla in a saucepan over medium heat. Bring to a boil and boil for 2 minutes, stirring constantly. Remove from the heat and let stand until cool. Pour over the cooled cake.

Tim White, Lebanon

Mom's Applesauce Cake

3 cups boiling water
1 pound seedless raisins
5 cups all-purpose flour
2 teaspoons baking soda
1 teaspoon baking powder
1 teaspoon ground cinnamon
1 teaspoon ground cloves
1 teaspoon nutmeg
1/2 teaspoon salt
1 cup (2 sticks) butter, softened
3 cups packed brown sugar
2 cups applesauce
1 cup chopped black walnuts

Pour the water over the raisins into a bowl. Let stand while preparing the remaining ingredients, stirring occasionally. Sift the flour, baking soda, baking powder, cinnamon, cloves, nutmeg and salt together. Cream the butter in a mixing bowl until fluffy. Add the brown sugar and applesauce and beat until smooth. Add the flour mixture gradually, stirring just until blended. Drain the raisins. Fold the raisins and walnuts into the cake batter. Spoon into a greased and floured 10-inch tube pan. Bake at 325 degrees for 1 3/4 hours or until a wooden pick inserted 1/2 inch from the side of the pan comes out clean. Cool in the pan for 15 minutes. Invert onto a wire rack to cool completely.

Barbara J. Bryant, Lebanon

Butter Pecan Banana Cake

CAKE

1 cup (2 sticks) butter or margarine, softened
1/2 cup shortening
2 cups firmly packed light brown sugar
1 cup granulated sugar
5 eggs
3 cups all-purpose flour
1/2 teaspoon baking powder
1/2 teaspoon baking soda
1/2 teaspoon salt
1/2 cup milk
2 large ripe bananas, mashed
1 cup chopped pecans
1 teaspoon vanilla extract

PECAN FROSTING

1/4 cup (1/2 stick) butter
1 cup coarsely chopped pecans
1/2 cup (1 stick) butter, softened
2 tablespoons milk
1 teaspoon vanilla extract
1 (1-pound) package confectioners' sugar

For the cake, beat the butter and shortening in a mixing bowl for 2 minutes or until creamy. Add the brown sugar and granulated sugar gradually, beating until blended. Beat the eggs 1 at a time. Mix the flour, baking powder, baking soda and salt in a bowl. Add to the creamed mixture alternately with the milk, beginning and ending with the flour mixture and beating well after each addition. Stir in the bananas, pecans and vanilla. Pour into a greased and floured 10-inch tube pan. Bake at 325 degrees for 65 minutes or until the cake tests done. Cool completely on a wire rack. Remove from the pan.

For the frosting, melt 1/4 cup butter in a skillet. Add the pecans and sauté until toasted. Remove from the heat and let cool completely. Cream 1/2 cup butter in a mixing bowl. Beat in the milk and vanilla. Add enough confectioners' sugar to make of a firm spreading consistency. Stir in the pecans. Spread over the top and sides of the cake.

Margaret Thompson Kilgore, Lebanon

Butternut Cake

CAKE
1 cup (2 sticks) butter or margarine, softened
2 cups sugar
1 cup buttermilk
1 teaspoon baking soda
1/4 teaspoon salt
3 cups sifted all-purpose flour
3 eggs, at room temperature
1 tablespoon butternut flavoring

BUTTERNUT FROSTING
1/2 cup (1 stick) butter or margarine, softened
8 ounces cream cheese, at room temperature
1 (1-pound) package confectioners' sugar
2 teaspoons butternut flavoring
1 cup chopped pecans

For the cake, cream the butter and sugar in a mixing bowl until light and fluffy. Combine the buttermilk, baking soda and salt in a mixing bowl and beat until foamy. Add to the creamed mixture alternately with the flour and eggs, mixing well after each addition. Add the butternut flavoring and mix well. Pour into three 9-inch round cake pans. Bake at 350 degrees for 30 minutes or until a wooden pick inserted in the center comes out clean. Cool in the pans for 10 minutes. Remove to wire racks to cool completely.

For the frosting, cream the butter and cream cheese in a mixing bowl. Add the confectioners' sugar gradually, beating constantly on low. Add the butternut flavoring and pecans and mix well. Spread between the layers and over the top and side of the cake.

Linda Saunders, Mt. Juliet

Pineapple Carrot Cake

CAKE

1 1/2 cups all-purpose flour
1 cup sugar
1 teaspoon baking powder
1 teaspoon baking soda
1 teaspoon ground cinnamon
1/2 teaspoon salt
2 eggs
2/3 cup vegetable oil
1 cup carrot baby food
1/2 cup crushed pineapple
1 teaspoon vanilla extract
1/2 cup chopped pecans

CREAM CHEESE FROSTING

8 ounces cream cheese, softened
2 tablespoons butter, softened
1 teaspoon vanilla extract
4 cups confectioners' sugar
Pecan halves

For the cake, sift the flour, sugar, baking powder, baking soda, cinnamon and salt together. Combine the eggs, oil, baby food, pineapple and vanilla in a mixing bowl and mix well. Add the flour mixture and beat at medium speed for 2 minutes. Stir in the pecans. Pour the batter into 2 greased and floured 8- or 9-inch round cake pans. Bake at 350 degrees for 30 minutes. Cool in the pans for 10 minutes. Remove to a wire rack and cool completely.

For the frosting, combine the cream cheese, butter and vanilla in a mixing bowl and beat until light and fluffy. Add the confectioners' sugar gradually, beating constantly. You may add a small amount of milk to reach the desired consistency. Spread between the layers and over the top and side of the cake. Decorate with pecan halves.

Denise Robinson, Lebanon

Carrot Cake

CAKE
2 cups twice-sifted all-purpose flour
2 teaspoons baking powder
2 teaspoons baking soda
1 teaspoon salt
2 teaspoons ground cinnamon
2 cups sugar
1$^1/_2$ cups vegetable oil
4 eggs
3 cups finely grated carrots
$^1/_2$ cup chopped nuts

BUTTERY CREAM CHEESE FROSTING
8 ounces cream cheese, softened
$^1/_4$ cup ($^1/_2$ stick) butter, softened
2 teaspoons vanilla extract
1 (1-pound) package confectioners' sugar

For the cake, sift the flour, baking powder, baking soda, salt and cinnamon together twice. Combine the sugar and oil in a mixing bowl and beat well. Add the eggs 1 at a time, beating well after each addition. Add the carrots and beat well. Add the flour mixture and mix well. Stir in the nuts. Pour into a greased and floured 8×12-inch cake pan. Bake at 300 degrees for 45 to 50 minutes or until the cake tests done. Let stand until cool.

For the frosting, combine the cream cheese, butter and vanilla in a mixing bowl and beat until blended. Add the confectioners' sugar and beat well. Spread over the cooled cake.

Sarah Jennings, Lebanon

Chocolate Cake

CAKE

2 cups sugar
1 3/4 cups all-purpose flour
3/4 cups baking cocoa
1 1/2 teaspoons baking powder
1 1/2 teaspoons baking soda
1 teaspoon salt
2 eggs
1 cup milk
1/2 cup vegetable oil
2 teaspoons vanilla extract
1 cup boiling water

CHOCOLATE FROSTING

1/2 cup (1 stick) butter
2/3 cup baking cocoa
3 cups confectioners' sugar
1/3 cup milk
1 teaspoon vanilla extract

For the cake, combine the sugar, flour, baking cocoa, baking powder, baking soda and salt in a large mixing bowl. Add the eggs, milk, oil and vanilla and beat at medium speed for 2 minutes. Stir in the water. The batter will be very thin. Pour into 2 greased and floured 9-inch round cake pans. Bake at 350 degrees for 30 to 35 minutes or until the cakes test done. Let cool completely.

For the frosting, melt the butter in a saucepan. Remove from the heat and let cool slightly. Pour into a mixing bowl and stir in the baking cocoa. Add the confectioners' sugar and milk alternately, beating at medium speed constantly and adding additional confectioners' sugar or milk to reach the desired consistency. Stir in the vanilla. Spread between the layers and over the top and side of the cooled cake.

Betty Weatherby, Lebanon

Chocolate Cake with Chocolate Cream Cheese Frosting

CAKE

1 cup hot water
1 cup mayonnaise
2 cups self-rising flour
1 1/2 cups sugar
3/4 cup baking cocoa

CHOCOLATE CREAM CHEESE FROSTING

8 ounces cream cheese, softened
1/4 cup (1/2 stick) margarine, softened
1 (1-pound) package confectioners' sugar
2 to 3 tablespoons milk

For the cake, combine the water, mayonnaise, flour, sugar and baking cocoa in a mixing bowl and beat at high speed until blended. Pour into 2 greased and floured 9-inch round cake pans. Bake at 350 degrees for 20 to 25 minutes or until the cakes test done. Let stand until cool.

For the frosting, combine the cream cheese, margarine and confectioners' sugar in a mixing bowl and beat at high speed until blended. Add the milk as needed to reach the desired consistency. Spread between the layers and over the top and side of the cooled cake.

Willette Piercey, Lebanon

Chocolate Fantasy Cake

CAKE

1 cup (2 sticks) butter, softened
2 cups sugar
2 eggs
1 teaspoon vanilla extract
3 cups sifted self-rising flour
1/2 cup baking cocoa
2 cups buttermilk
1/2 cup ground pecans

CHOCOLATE GLAZE

2 cups (12 ounces) semisweet chocolate chips
1/3 cup butter
1/4 cup chopped pecans

WHITE CHOCOLATE GLAZE

1/2 cup (3 ounces) white chocolate chips
1 tablespoon shortening

For the cake, cream the butter in a mixing bowl. Add the sugar gradually, beating constantly until fluffy. Add the eggs 1 at a time, beating well after each addition. Add the vanilla and mix well. Combine the flour and baking cocoa in a bowl. Add to the creamed mixture alternately with the buttermilk, beating at low speed constantly. Stir in the pecans. Pour into a greased and floured bundt pan. Bake at 350 degrees for 45 minutes or until a wooden pick inserted in the center comes out clean. Cool in the pan for 15 minutes. Invert onto a serving plate and cool completely.

For the chocolate glaze, melt the chocolate chips and butter in a small heavy saucepan over low heat, stirring constantly until the mixture is shiny and smooth. Add additional butter for a thinner glaze. Pour the hot glaze over the cooled cake. Sprinkle with the pecans.

For the white chocolate glaze, melt the white chocolate chips and shortening in a small heavy saucepan over low heat, stirring constantly until blended. Add additional shortening for a thinner glaze. Drizzle over the top and side of the cake.

Leasa Gammon, Lebanon

Cocoa Pecan Cake

CAKE

2 cups sifted all-purpose flour
2 cups sugar
1 teaspoon baking soda
1/2 teaspoon salt
1 cup (2 sticks) butter or margarine
6 tablespoons baking cocoa
1 cup water
2 eggs
1 cup sour cream

CHOCOLATE PECAN FROSTING

1/2 cup (1 stick) butter or margarine
6 tablespoons milk
1/4 cup baking cocoa
1 (1-pound) package confectioners' sugar
1 teaspoon vanilla extract
1 cup chopped pecans

For the cake, combine the flour, sugar, baking soda and salt in a bowl. Melt the butter in a saucepan. Add the baking cocoa and water and bring to a boil, stirring constantly until blended. Pour the mixture into a mixing bowl. Add the flour mixture, eggs and sour cream alternately, beating well after each addition. Pour into a 9×13-inch cake pan. Bake at 350 degrees for 30 minutes or until a wooden pick inserted in the center comes out clean.

For the frosting, combine the butter, milk and baking cocoa in a saucepan and heat just until boiling, stirring until blended. Remove from the heat. Add the confectioners' sugar, vanilla and pecans and mix well. Spread the warm frosting over the warm cake.

Linda Saunders, Mt. Juliet

Lovelight Chocolate Cake

CAKE

2 egg whites
1/2 cup sugar
13/4 cups cake flour
1 cup sugar
3/4 teaspoon baking soda
3/4 teaspoon salt
1/3 cup vegetable oil
1/2 cup buttermilk
2 egg yolks
2 ounces semisweet chocolate, melted and cooled
1/2 cup buttermilk

CHOCOLATE CREAM CHEESE FROSTING

3 tablespoons butter, softened
3 ounces cream cheese, softened
4 cups confectioners' sugar
3 to 4 tablespoons milk
2 ounces semisweet chocolate, melted and cooled
1 teaspoon vanilla extract

For the cake, beat the egg whites in a mixing bowl until stiff peaks form. Add 1/2 cup sugar gradually, beating constantly until stiff peaks form. Combine the flour, 1 cup sugar, the baking soda and salt in a mixing bowl. Add the oil and 1/2 cup buttermilk and beat for 1 minute. Add the egg yolks, chocolate and 1/2 cup buttermilk and beat for 1 minute. Fold in the egg white mixture. Pour into 2 greased 9-inch round cake pans. Bake at 350 degrees for 30 to 35 minutes or until the cakes test done. Cool in the pans for 10 minutes. Remove to a wire rack to cool completely.

For the frosting, cream the butter and cream cheese in a mixing bowl. Add the confectioners' sugar alternately with the milk, mixing well after each addition. Add the chocolate and vanilla gradually, mixing constantly. Spread between the layers and over the top and side of the cooled cake. Chill, covered, before serving.

Margaret Thompson Kilgore, Lebanon

Mama's Chocolate Cake

CAKE
$1^1/_2$ cups self-rising flour
$1^1/_4$ cups sugar
2 heaping tablespoons baking cocoa
$^1/_2$ cup milk
$^1/_2$ cup shortening
2 eggs
6 tablespoons milk
1 teaspoon vanilla extract

FUDGE ICING
2 cups sugar
$^1/_2$ cup milk
$^1/_2$ cup (1 stick) butter
2 heaping tablespoons baking cocoa

For the cake, combine the flour, sugar and baking cocoa in a mixing bowl. Add $^1/_2$ cup milk and mix well. Add the shortening, eggs and 6 tablespoons milk and beat at medium speed for 2 minutes. Stir in the vanilla. Pour into a greased 9×13-inch cake pan or 2 greased 9-inch round cake pans. Bake at 350 degrees for 25 minutes. Cool on wire racks.

For the icing, combine the sugar, milk, butter and baking cocoa in a saucepan. Bring to a rolling boil. Boil for 2 minutes, stirring frequently. Pour into a mixing bowl and beat until cool. Spread over the top of the 9×13-inch cake or between the layers and over the top and side of the cake layers.

Scott Hobbs, Lebanon

Turtle Cake

CAKE

$1\frac{1}{2}$ cups (9 ounces) semisweet chocolate chips
$\frac{1}{2}$ cup (1 stick) butter, softened
1 (1-pound) package light brown sugar
3 eggs
2 cups all-purpose flour
1 teaspoon baking soda
$\frac{1}{2}$ teaspoon salt
1 cup sour cream
1 cup hot water
2 teaspoons vanilla extract

CARAMEL FILLING

1 cup (2 sticks) butter
2 cups sugar
2 tablespoons corn syrup
1 cup heavy cream or whipping cream

CHOCOLATE GANACHE

2 cups (12 ounces) semisweet chocolate chips
$\frac{1}{2}$ cup heavy cream or whipping cream
3 tablespoons butter

ASSEMBLY

1 cup chopped pecans

For the cake, microwave the chocolate in a microwave-safe bowl on High until melted and smooth, stirring at 30-second intervals. Combine the butter and brown sugar in a mixing bowl and beat for 5 minutes or until blended. Add the eggs 1 at a time, beating well after each addition. Add the melted chocolate and beat until blended. Sift the flour, baking soda and salt together. Add to the chocolate mixture alternately with the sour cream, beginning and ending with the flour mixture and beating at low speed just until blended after each addition. Add the hot water in a steady stream, beating constantly until blended. Stir in the vanilla. Spoon into 3 greased and floured 9-inch round cake pans. Bake at 350 degrees for 25 to 30 minutes or until a wooden pick inserted in the centers comes out clean. Cool in the pans on wire racks for 10 minutes. Remove to wire racks to cool completely.

For the caramel filling, melt the butter in a heavy 3-quart saucepan over medium heat. Add the sugar and corn syrup and cook for 6 to 8 minutes or until the mixture turns a deep caramel color, stirring constantly. Add the cream gradually, stirring constantly for 1 to 2 minutes or until smooth. Remove from the heat and let stand until cool. Chill, covered, for 2 hours or until thickened and of a spreading consistency.

For the ganache, combine the chocolate and cream in a microwave-safe bowl. Microwave on Medium for 2 to 3 minutes or until the chocolate begins to melt. Whisk until the chocolate is melted and the mixture is smooth. Add the butter and stir until blended. Let stand for 20 minutes. Beat at medium speed for 3 to 4 minutes or until soft peaks form.

For the assembly, place 1 cake layer on a serving plate. Spread 1 cup of the caramel filling over the top. Sprinkle with 1/3 cup of the pecans. Repeat the layering procedure with the remaining cake layers, filling and pecans. Spread the ganache evenly over the side of the cake.

Amy Upchurch, Watertown

Coconut Cake

CAKE

1 cup (2 sticks) butter, at room temperature
2 cups sugar
4 eggs
3 cups sifted self-rising flour
1 cup coconut milk
1 teaspoon vanilla extract

FILLING

3/4 cup sugar
1/2 cup sweetened coconut flakes
1 cup sour cream
1/4 cup milk

VANILLA FROSTING

1 1/2 cups sugar
1/4 teaspoon cream of tartar,
or 1 tablespoon white corn syrup
1/8 teaspoon salt
2 egg whites
1/3 cup water
1 1/2 teaspoons vanilla extract
Sweetened coconut flakes

For the cake, cream the butter in a mixing bowl until fluffy. Add the sugar and beat for 6 to 8 minutes or until light and fluffy. Add the eggs 1 at a time, beating well after each addition. Add the flour and coconut milk alternately, beginning and ending with the flour. Add the vanilla and beat just until combined. Pour the batter evenly into 3 greased and floured 9-inch round cake pans. Level and release air bubbles in the batter in each pan by tapping the bottoms of the pans gently on the kitchen counter. Bake at 350 degrees for 25 to 30 minutes or until the cakes test done. Cool in the pans for 5 to 10 minutes. Invert the cakes onto wire racks to cool completely.

For the filling, combine the sugar, coconut, sour cream and milk in a bowl and mix well.

For the frosting, combine the sugar, cream of tartar, salt, egg whites and water in the top of a double boiler. Beat with a hand-held mixer for 1 minute. Place the pan over boiling water, being sure that the water does not touch the bottom of the top pan. Beat at high speed with an electric mixer for 7 minutes. Beat in the vanilla.

For the assembly, place 1 cake layer on a cake plate. Poke holes 1 inch apart in the cake layer using the handle of a wooden spoon. Spread 1/2 of the filling over the cake layer. Top with a cake layer and repeat the procedure with the remaining filling and remaining cake layer. Spread the frosting over the top and side of the cake. Sprinkle with coconut.

Amy Upchurch, Watertown

Buttermilk Coconut Cake

CAKE

2 cups all-purpose flour
1 teaspoon baking powder
1/2 teaspoon baking soda
1/8 teaspoon salt
1/2 cup shortening or margarine
1 3/4 cups sugar
1 teaspoon vanilla extract
4 egg whites
1 1/3 cups buttermilk

CREAM CHEESE ICING

8 ounces cream cheese, softened
1/2 cup (1 stick) margarine
2 teaspoons vanilla extract
2 cups confectioners' sugar
1 (7-ounce) package flaked coconut

For the cake, combine the flour, baking powder, baking soda and salt in a bowl. Cream the shortening in a mixing bowl. Add the sugar and vanilla and beat until blended. Add the egg whites 1 at a time, beating well after each addition. Add the flour mixture and buttermilk alternately, beating at low speed constantly. Pour into 2 lightly greased 9-inch round cake pans. Bake at 350 degrees for 35 minutes or until a wooden pick inserted in the centers comes out clean. Let stand until cool.

For the icing, cream the cream cheese and margarine in a mixing bowl. Add the vanilla and mix well. Add the confectioners' sugar, beating until blended and of the desired spreading consistency. Spread between the layers and over the top and side of the cooled cake. Sprinkle the coconut over the top and side of the cake.

Betty Weatherby, Lebanon

Coconut Cake with Seven-Minute Frosting

CAKE

4 eggs, beaten
2 cups sugar
1 cup vegetable oil
1 cup (2 sticks) butter, softened
2 cups self-rising flour
1 tablespoon vanilla extract

SEVEN-MINUTE FROSTING

1/2 cup sugar
1/4 teaspoon cream of tartar
2 egg whites
1/3 cup water
2 teaspoons corn syrup
Dash of salt
1 teaspoon vanilla extract
1 (7-ounce) package flaked coconut

For the cake, combine the eggs, sugar, oil and butter in a mixing bowl and beat until blended. Add the flour and mix well. Stir in the vanilla. Pour into 2 greased and floured 9-inch round cake pans. Bake at 400 degrees for 45 to 50 minutes or until the cakes test done. Let stand until cool.

For the frosting, combine the sugar, cream of tartar, egg whites, water, corn syrup and salt in the top of a double boiler and beat for a few seconds or until blended. Place over boiling water and cook for 7 minutes or until very stiff, stirring constantly. Add the vanilla and beat for 1 minute. Spread the frosting between the layers and over the top and side of the cake. Sprinkle the coconut over the top and side of the cake.

Betty Weatherby, Lebanon

Coconut Dream Cake

CAKE

2$^{1}/_{4}$ cups all-purpose flour
1$^{1}/_{3}$ cups sugar
1 tablespoon baking powder
$^{1}/_{2}$ teaspoon salt
$^{1}/_{2}$ cup shortening
1 cup low-fat milk
1 teaspoon vanilla extract
2 teaspoons coconut flavoring
2 eggs

COCONUT FROSTING AND ASSEMBLY

1 cup sour cream
12 ounces frozen flaked coconut, thawed
2 cups sugar
2 cups whipped topping
Toasted flaked coconut (optional)

For the cake, combine the flour, sugar, baking powder and salt in a mixing bowl. Add the shortening, milk, vanilla and coconut flavoring and beat until blended. Add the eggs 1 at a time, beating well after each addition. Pour into 2 greased and floured 8-inch round cake pans. Bake at 350 degrees for 30 to 35 minutes or until a wooden pick inserted in the centers comes out clean. Cool completely on wire racks.

For the frosting and assembly, combine the sour cream, coconut and sugar in a bowl and mix well. Chill, covered, while the cake is baking and cooling. Cut the cake layers horizontally into halves. Reserve 1$^{1}/_{2}$ cups of the coconut mixture. Spread the remaining coconut mixture between the cake layers. Combine the reserved coconut mixture and the whipped topping in a bowl and mix well. Spread over the top and side of the cake. Sprinkle with toasted coconut. Place the cake in an airtight container and refrigerate for 3 days before serving. Keep refrigerated.

Margaret Thompson Kilgore, Lebanon

Sour Cream Coconut Cake

CAKE

1 cup shortening
2 cups sugar
$1^1/_2$ teaspoons salt
$3^3/_4$ cups all-purpose flour
4 teaspoons baking powder
$1^1/_2$ cups water
2 teaspoons vanilla extract
7 egg whites
$^1/_2$ cup sugar

COCONUT ICING

4 cups sugar
$1^1/_2$ cups sour cream
1 (24-ounce) package flaked coconut
8 ounces whipped topping

For the cake, cream the shortening, 2 cups sugar and the salt in a mixing bowl. Sift together the flour and baking powder twice. Stir the water and vanilla into the flour mixture. Add the flour mixture to the creamed mixture and mix well. Beat the egg whites in a mixing bowl until soft peaks form. Add $^1/_2$ cup sugar and beat until stiff peaks form. Fold the egg whites into the batter. Pour into three 8-inch round cake pans. Bake at 375 degrees for 25 minutes or until the cakes test done. Let stand until cool. Cut the cooled cake layers horizontally into halves.

For the icing, combine the sugar and sour cream in a bowl and mix well. Add the coconut and mix well. Reserve $1^1/_2$ cups of the mixture. Spread the remaining mixture between the cake layers. Add the whipped topping to the reserved coconut mixture. Spread over the top and side of the cake. Chill until ready to serve. This is better if prepared and chilled 1 day in advance.

Lisa Rollins, Lebanon

Praline Pecan Cornmeal Cake

CAKE

1 cup (2 sticks) margarine, softened
1 1/4 cups granulated sugar
3/4 cup packed light brown sugar
5 eggs
1 cup sour cream
2 1/4 cups all-purpose flour
1/2 cup cornmeal
2 teaspoons baking powder
1 teaspoon salt
1 1/3 teaspoons ground cinnamon
1 cup chopped pecans

BROWN SUGAR PECAN GLAZE

1/2 cup (1 stick) butter
1 (1-pound) package brown sugar
2 cups heavy cream or whipping cream
1 cup pecans

For the cake, cream the margarine, granulated sugar and brown sugar in a mixing bowl. Add the eggs 1 at a time, beating constantly until light and fluffy. Beat in the sour cream. Add the flour, cornmeal, baking powder, salt and cinnamon and beat until blended. Stir in the pecans. Pour into a greased cast iron skillet. Bake at 325 degrees or until a knife inserted in the center comes out clean.

For the glaze, melt the butter in a heavy skillet. Add the brown sugar and stir until dissolved. Cook for 1 minute. Stir in the cream and pecans. Pour over the cake.

Willette Piercey, Lebanon

Old-Fashioned Pound Cake

3 cups all-purpose flour
2 cups sugar
1 tablespoon baking powder
1/2 teaspoon salt
2 cups (4 sticks) butter, softened
1/2 cup low-fat milk
1 teaspoon vanilla extract
1 teaspoon almond extract
6 eggs

Combine the flour, sugar, baking powder and salt in a large mixing bowl. Combine the butter, milk and flavorings in a bowl and mix well. Add to the flour mixture and beat until blended. Add the eggs 1 at a time, beating well after each addition. Pour the batter into 2 greased and floured 10-inch tube pans. Bake at 350 degrees for 1 1/4 hours or until a wooden pick inserted in the centers comes out clean. Cool completely on wire racks. Remove from the pans.

Margaret Thompson Kilgore, Lebanon

Seven-Up Pound Cake

1 cup (2 sticks) butter, softened
1/2 cup shortening
3 cups sugar
5 eggs
3 cups sifted all-purpose flour
1 teaspoon vanilla extract
1 teaspoon lemon flavoring
1 small bottle 7-Up

Cream the butter, shortening and sugar in mixing bowl. Add the eggs 1 at a time, beating well after each addition. Add the flour gradually, beating constantly. Stir in the flavorings. Add the 7-Up gradually, stirring to combine. Do not beat. Pour into a tube pan. Bake at 325 degrees for 1 hour and 10 minutes. Let stand for 15 minutes. Remove from the pan to cool completely.

Brenda Cline, Mt. Juliet

Sour Cream Pound Cake

$1^1/_2$ cups (3 sticks) butter, softened
3 cups sugar
6 eggs
3 cups all-purpose flour
1 teaspoon vanilla extract
1 cup sour cream

Cream the butter and sugar in a mixing bowl. Add the eggs 1 at a time, beating well after each addition. Add the flour and beat until blended. Add the vanilla and sour cream and mix well. Pour into a tube pan. Bake at 325 degrees for $1^1/_2$ hours.

Sue Eaton, Lebanon

Pound Cake

1 cup (2 sticks) butter, softened
2 cups sugar
4 eggs
3 cups all-purpose flour
$^1/_2$ teaspoon vanilla extract

Cream the butter and sugar in a mixing bowl. Add the eggs 1 at a time, beating well after each addition. Add the flour and vanilla and beat at high speed for 5 minutes. Pour into a tube pan. Bake at 325 degrees for 45 minutes.

Ed Eaton, Lebanon

Red Velvet Cake

CAKE

1/2 cup shortening
1 1/2 cups sugar
2 eggs, beaten
1 teaspoon salt
1 cup buttermilk
2 1/2 cups sifted cake flour
2 ounces red food coloring
2 teaspoons baking cocoa
1 teaspoon vanilla extract
1 teaspoon baking soda
1 tablespoon white vinegar

CREAM CHEESE FROSTING

1/2 cup (1 stick) margarine, softened
8 ounces cream cheese, softened
1 (1-pound) package confectioners' sugar
Chopped pecans

For the cake, cream the shortening and sugar in a mixing bowl. Add the eggs, salt and buttermilk and beat until blended. Add the flour and mix well. Combine the food coloring, baking cocoa and vanilla in a small bowl and mix until of a paste consistency. Stir into the batter. Combine the baking soda and vinegar in a small bowl and mix well. Stir into the batter. Do not beat. Pour into 3 well-greased 8- or 9-inch round cake pans. Bake at 350 degrees for 35 minutes. Let cool completely.

For the frosting, combine the margarine, cream cheese and confectioners' sugar in a mixing bowl and beat until blended and of a spreading consistency. Spread between the layers and over the top and side of the cake. Sprinkle with pecans.

Cindy Mangrum, Lebanon

Red Cross Red Velvet Cake

CAKE

2 1/2 cups all-purpose flour
1 1/2 cups sugar
1 teaspoon baking soda
1 teaspoon salt
2 teaspoons baking cocoa
1 1/2 cups vegetable oil
1 cup buttermilk, at room temperature
2 eggs, at room temperature
2 1/2 tablespoons red food coloring
1 teaspoon white vinegar
1 teaspoon vanilla extract

CREAM CHEESE FROSTING

16 ounces cream cheese, softened
1 cup (2 sticks) unsalted butter, softened
4 cups sifted confectioners' sugar
1 teaspoon vanilla extract

For the cake, combine the flour, sugar, baking soda, salt and baking cocoa in a bowl. Combine the oil, buttermilk, eggs, food coloring, vinegar and vanilla in the bowl of a standing mixer and whisk until blended. Add the flour mixture and beat with the paddle attachment until blended and smooth. Pour into 2 lightly greased and floured 9-inch round cake pans. Bake at 350 degrees for 25 to 30 minutes or until the cakes begin to pull away from the sides of the pans and a wooden pick inserted in the centers comes out clean, rotating the pans halfway through the baking process. Invert the cakes onto a plate. Invert the cakes onto a wire rack to cool completely.

For the frosting, place the cream cheese, butter and confectioners' sugar in the bowl of a standing mixer and beat at low speed just until combined. Beat at high speed for 5 minutes or until light and fluffy. Reduce the speed to low and add the vanilla. Increase the speed to high and beat until fluffy. Chill, covered, in the refrigerator until the batter becomes slightly stiff. Spread between the layers and over the top and side of the cake.

Mary Pitcock, Lebanon

Red Velvet Cake with Cream Cheese Frosting

CAKE

2 1/2 cups sugar
1 1/2 cups vegetable oil
1 1/2 cups all-purpose flour
1 tablespoon baking cocoa
1 teaspoon baking soda
1 teaspoon salt
1 1/2 cups buttermilk
3 eggs
1 teaspoon vanilla extract
1 teaspoon white vinegar
2 ounces red food coloring

CREAM CHEESE FROSTING

8 ounces cream cheese, softened
1/2 cup (1 stick) butter or margarine, softened
1 (1-pound) package confectioners' sugar
1 cup chopped pecans (optional)

For the cake, combine the sugar and oil in a bowl and mix well. Combine the flour, baking cocoa, baking soda and salt in a mixing bowl. Add the sugar mixture and beat until blended. Add the buttermilk and beat well. Add the eggs 1 at a time, beating after each addition. Beat in the vanilla and vinegar. Add the food coloring and beat until blended. Pour into 3 greased and floured 8- or 9-inch round cake pans. Bake at 350 degrees for 25 to 30 minutes or until the cakes spring back when touched in the center. Cool on wire racks.

For the frosting, beat the cream cheese and butter in a mixing bowl until blended. Add the confectioners' sugar and mix well. Stir in the pecans. Spread between the layers and over the top and side of the cake.

Ellen Hooper, Lebanon

Red Velvet Cake with Cream Cheese Marshmallow Frosting

CAKE

2 1/2 cups cake flour
1 teaspoon salt
1 cup (2 sticks) butter, at room temperature
2 cups sugar
2 eggs
2 tablespoons baking cocoa
2 ounces red food coloring
1 cup buttermilk
1 teaspoon vanilla extract
1/2 teaspoon baking soda
1 tablespoon white vinegar

CREAM CHEESE MARSHMALLOW FROSTING

8 ounces cream cheese, softened
1/2 cup (1 stick) butter, softened
1 cup melted marshmallows
1 (1-pound) package confectioners' sugar
1 cup finely chopped pecans

For the cake, sift the flour and salt together. Cream the butter in a mixing bowl. Add the sugar and beat until light and fluffy. Add the eggs 1 at a time, beating well after each addition. Combine the baking cocoa and food coloring in a small bowl and mix well. Add to the sugar mixture and mix well. Add the flour mixture alternately with the buttermilk, beating well after each addition. Add the vanilla and beat until blended. Combine the baking soda and vinegar in a small bowl and mix well. Stir into the batter. Pour into 3 greased and floured 8-inch round cake pans. Bake at 350 degrees for 20 to 25 minutes or until a wooden pick inserted in the centers comes out clean. Let cool completely.

For the frosting, cream the cream cheese and butter in a mixing bowl. Add the marshmallows and confectioners' sugar and beat until blended. Fold in the pecans. Spread between the layers and over the top and side of the cake.

Leasa Gammon, Lebanon

Chocolate Truffle Cheesecake

CRUST

$1^1/_2$ cups crushed chocolate sandwich cookies (about 21 cookies)
$^1/_4$ cup ($^1/_2$ stick) butter or margarine, melted

FILLING

24 ounces cream cheese, softened
$1^1/_4$ cups sugar
3 eggs
1 cup sour cream
1 teaspoon vanilla extract

8 ounces cream cheese, softened
1 cup (6 ounces) semisweet chocolate chips, melted
$^1/_3$ cup seedless raspberry preserves

TOPPING

2 cups sour cream
$^1/_4$ cup sugar
1 teaspoon vanilla extract

CHOCOLATE SAUCE

$^1/_2$ cup (3 ounces) semisweet chocolate chips
$^1/_4$ cup heavy cream or whipping cream

For the crust, combine the cookie crumbs and butter in a bowl and mix well. Press in the bottom of a 10-inch springform pan. Bake at 400 degrees for 8 minutes. Cool on a wire rack.

For the filling, beat 24 ounces cream cheese at medium speed in a mixing bowl until creamy. Add the sugar gradually, beating constantly. Add the eggs 1 at a time, beating well after each addition. Stir in the sour cream and vanilla. Combine 8 ounces cream cheese, the melted chocolate and raspberry preserves in a bowl and mix well. Spoon 2/3 of the sour cream mixture over the prepared crust. Drop the chocolate mixture by rounded tablespoonfuls over the batter. Pour the remaining sour cream mixture over the chocolate. Bake at 325 degrees for 1 hour 20 minutes or until almost set. The cheesecake will rise above the pan. Increase the temperature to 375 degrees.

For the topping, combine the sour cream, sugar and vanilla in a bowl and mix well. Spread over the cheesecake. Bake for 5 minutes. Cool on a wire rack. Chill, covered, in the refrigerator for 8 hours.

For the chocolate sauce, combine the chocolate chips and cream in a saucepan over low heat. Cook until the chocolate melts, stirring constantly. Remove the side of the springform pan. Slice the cheesecake. Drizzle each slice with the chocolate sauce. Garnish with whipped cream, fresh raspberries and mint sprigs.

Amy Upchurch, Watertown

Chocolate Raspberry Cheesecake

CRUST

18 chocolate sandwich cookies, finely crushed
2 tablespoons butter, softened

FILLING

24 ounces cream cheese, softened
3/4 cup sugar
1 teaspoon vanilla extract
3 eggs
1/2 cup sour cream

8 ounces cream cheese, softened
6 ounces semisweet baking chocolate, melted
1/3 cup raspberry preserves

CHOCOLATE SAUCE

6 ounces semisweet baking chocolate
1/4 cup heavy cream or whipping cream

For the crust, combine the cookie crumbs and butter in a bowl and mix well. Press in the bottom of a 9-inch springform pan.

For the filling, combine 24 ounces cream cheese, the sugar and vanilla in a mixing bowl and beat until blended. Add the eggs 1 at a time, beating well after each addition. Beat in the sour cream. Pour over the crust. Beat 8 ounces cream cheese and the chocolate in a mixing bowl until blended. Add the preserves and mix well. Drop by rounded tablespoonfuls over the cream cheese batter. Bake at 325 degrees for 1 hour and 15 minutes to 1 hour and 20 minutes or until the center is almost set. Run a knife or metal spatula around the rim of the pan to loosen the cheesecake. Let cool in the pan. Remove the side of the pan.

For the chocolate sauce, heat the chocolate and cream in a saucepan over low heat until the chocolate is melted, stirring constantly until smooth. Spread over the cooled cheesecake. Chill in the refrigerator for 4 to 8 hours. Garnish with whipped cream and fresh raspberries.

Theda K. Rose, Lebanon

Classic Italian Cheesecake

CRUST

1 1/4 cups vanilla wafer crumbs
3 tablespoons butter, melted

FILLING

4 cups light ricotta cheese
3/4 cup sugar
1/2 cup half-and-half
1/4 cup all-purpose flour
1 teaspoon vanilla extract
1/4 teaspoon salt
3 eggs

For the crust, combine the cookie crumbs and butter in a bowl and mix well. Press in the bottom of a lightly greased 8- or 9-inch springform pan. Chill in the refrigerator.

For the filling, combine the ricotta cheese, sugar, half-and-half, flour, vanilla and salt in a mixing bowl and beat until smooth. Add the eggs 1 at a time, beating after each addition until smooth. Pour over the crust. Bake at 350 degrees for 1 hour or just until the center is set. Turn off the oven. Let cheesecake stand in the oven with the door propped open for 30 minutes. Remove to a wire rack Run a metal spatula around the rim of the pan to loosen the cheesecake and let cool completely. Chill for 4 hours or longer before serving.

Theda K. Rose, Lebanon

Dulce de Leche Cheesecake

CRUST

1 1/3 cups graham cracker crumbs
1/4 cup crushed walnuts
1/3 cup butter or margarine, melted

FILLING

1 (6-ounce) package chocolate-covered chocolate caramels
1 tablespoon milk
1 envelope unflavored gelatin
1/4 cup rum (preferably dark) or milk
24 ounces cream cheese, at room temperature
1 (14-ounce) can sweetened condensed milk
1 3/4 cups whipped topping or whipped cream

TOPPING

1 cup whipped topping or heavy cream or whipping cream, whipped
15 caramels, melted
Mini-crunch candy bars, quartered diagonally (optional)

For the crust, combine the graham cracker crumbs, walnuts and butter in a bowl and mix well. Press in the bottom and up the side of an 8-inch springform pan sprayed with nonstick cooking spray. Freeze for 10 minutes.

For the filling, combine the chocolate caramels with the milk in a microwave-safe bowl. Microwave at 10-second intervals until melted, stirring until smooth. Pour evenly over the crust. Chill in the refrigerator. Sprinkle the gelatin over the rum in a microwave-safe bowl. Let stand for 5 minutes. Microwave at 5-second intervals until warm, stirring until smooth.

Beat the cream cheese at medium speed in a mixing bowl for 4 minutes or until fluffy. Beat in the condensed milk. Add the gelatin mixture gradually, beating constantly at low speed. Beat at high speed for 1 minute or until blended. Fold in the whipped topping. Pour over the prepared layer. Chill, covered, for 6 hours or longer. Remove the side of the pan.

For the topping, spoon the whipped topping into a pastry bag fitted with a large star tip. Pipe onto the cheesecake. Drizzle with the melted caramels. Top with the candy bar pieces.

Carol Swope, Lebanon

Plain Ole Cheesecake

CRUST

1 cup crushed vanilla wafers
1/4 cup (1/2 stick) butter, melted

FILLING

32 ounces cream cheese, softened
2 cups sugar
1 teaspoon vanilla extract
4 eggs

For the crust, combine the cookie crumbs and butter in a bowl and mix well. Press in the bottom of a 9-inch springform pan. Chill for 20 minutes.

For the filling, combine the cream cheese, sugar and vanilla in a mixing bowl and beat until blended. Add the eggs 1 at a time, beating well after each addition. Pour over the prepared crust. Bake at 325 degrees for 1 hour or until light brown. Run a knife around the rim of the pan to loosen the cheesecake. Refrigerate for 6 hours before serving.

Barry Tatum, Lebanon

King Kamehameha Cheesecake

CRUST
1 cup crushed vanilla wafers
1/4 cup (1/2 stick) butter, melted

FILLING
32 ounces cream cheese, softened
2 cups sugar
3 tablespoons milk
4 eggs
1 cup toasted macadamia nuts
1 cup shredded coconut

TOPPING
1 (8-ounce) can crushed pineapple, drained
1 kiwifruit, peeled and sliced

For the crust, combine the cookie crumbs and butter in a bowl and mix well. Press in the bottom of a 9-inch springform pan. Chill in the refrigerator for 20 minutes.

For the filling, combine the cream cheese, sugar and milk in a mixing bowl and beat until blended. Add the eggs 1 at a time, beating well after each addition. Stir in the macadamia nuts and coconut. Bake at 325 degrees for 1 hour or until light brown.

For the topping, spread the pineapple over the top of the cheesecake. Broil just until the pineapple begins to brown. Run a knife around the rim of the pan to loosen the cheesecake. Chill for 6 hours. Remove the side of the pan and top with the kiwifruit.

Barry Tatum, Lebanon

New York Cheesecake

CRUST
1 cup graham cracker crumbs
3 tablespoons sugar
3 tablespoons butter, melted

FILLING
1 cup sugar
3 tablespoons all-purpose flour
32 ounces cream cheese, softened
4 eggs
1 cup sour cream
1 teaspoon vanilla extract

For the crust, combine the graham cracker crumbs, sugar and butter in a bowl and mix well. Press in the bottom of a springform pan. Bake at 350 degrees for 8 minutes.

For the filling, combine the sugar and flour in a bowl. Combine the cream cheese and eggs in a mixing bowl and beat until blended. Add the sugar mixture gradually, beating constantly until blended. Add the sour cream and vanilla and beat well. Pour over the prepared crust. Bake at 325 degrees for 1 hour. Run a knife around the rim of the pan to loosen the cheesecake. Let cool completely. Chill in the refrigerator until ready to serve.

Joy Adams, Lebanon

White Chocolate Cheesecake

CRUST

2 cups crushed chocolate wafers
1/2 cup (1 stick) butter or margarine, melted

FILLING

2 cups small curd cottage cheese
16 ounces cream cheese, softened
1 1/3 cups sugar
4 eggs
1/3 cup cornstarch
2 tablespoons lemon juice
1 teaspoon vanilla extract
1/2 cup (1 stick) butter or margarine, melted
2 cups sour cream
8 ounces white chocolate, melted

For the crust, combine the cookie crumbs and butter in a bowl and mix well. Press in the bottom of a springform pan.

For the filling, combine the cottage cheese and cream cheese in a mixing bowl and beat until blended. Add the sugar, eggs, cornstarch, lemon juice and vanilla and beat well. Beat in the butter, sour cream and white chocolate. Pour over the prepared crust. Bake at 325 degrees for 1 hour and 10 minutes. Do not open the oven door. Turn the oven off and let the cheesecake stand in the closed oven for 2 hours. Remove to a wire rack to cool completely. Chill in the refrigerator. Remove the side of the pan. Garnish with fresh berries. The cheesecake may be frozen.

Robyn Erickson, Lebanon

Candy

Divinity

2 cups sugar
1 cup water
1/2 cup white corn syrup
2 egg whites, at room temperature
1/2 teaspoon vanilla extract

Mix the sugar, water and corn syrup in a microwave-safe dish and cover with waxed paper. Microwave on High for 6 minutes. Uncover and microwave for 10 minutes longer. Beat the egg whites and vanilla in a mixing bowl until stiff peaks form. Add the hot mixture gradually, beating constantly for 5 minutes. Drop by spoonfuls onto waxed paper. Let stand until cool. You may add nuts or cherries, if desired.

Willette Piercy, Lebanon

Cordial Cherries

1 (10-ounce) jar maraschino cherries with stems
1 tablespoon brandy extract
6 ounces semisweet chocolate, chopped

Remove 1 tablespoon of the cherry juice from the jar of cherries and add the brandy extract. Freeze for 8 to 12 hours or soak for 3 days or longer.

Place the chocolate in a microwave-safe dish. Microwave on High for 1 minute and stir. Continue to microwave at 10-second intervals until the chocolate is melted but not hot, stirring after each interval.

Drain the cherries. Dip the cherries 1 at a time into the melted chocolate and swirl to coat. Place on a tray lined with waxed paper and chill until set.

Rachel Gregory, Lebanon

Chocolate Mice

1 (10-ounce) jar maraschino cherries with stems
6 blocks of chocolate candy coating
2 tablespoons shortening
Almond slivers

Drain the cherries and place on paper towels to dry. Melt the candy coating and shortening in a double boiler. Roll around the cherries and insert the almond slivers to resemble ears. The stem of the cherries will be the tail. Dip into the chocolate mixture, letting the excess drip off. Place on waxed paper and let stand until set.

Willette Piercy, Lebanon

Chocolate Marshmallow Creme Fudge

3/4 cup (1 1/2 sticks) margarine
3 cups sugar
1 (5-ounce) can evaporated milk
2 cups (12 ounces) semisweet chocolate chips
1 (7-ounce) jar marshmallow creme
1 teaspoon vanilla extract
1 cup chopped nuts (optional)

Microwave the margarine in a microwave-safe dish on High until mostly melted. Combine the melted margarine, sugar and evaporated milk in a lightly greased 4-quart saucepan. Bring to a full rolling boil over medium heat, stirring constantly. Continue to boil for 5 minutes. Remove from the heat. Stir in the chocolate chips gradually until melted. Add the marshmallow creme and vanilla and mix well. Stir in the nuts. Pour into a lightly greased pan. Cool completely before cutting into squares.

Russell Lane, Lebanon

Chocolate Fudge

1/2 cup (1 stick) margarine
2 cups sugar
3 tablespoons baking cocoa
1/2 cup milk
1 teaspoon vanilla extract

Melt the margarine in a saucepan over low heat. Add the sugar, baking cocoa and milk and bring to a boil. Boil for 2 minutes. Remove from the heat. Add the vanilla and beat until smooth. Pour into a pan sprayed with nonstick cooking spray. Cool completely before cutting into squares.

Mary Lou Ford, Lebanon

Chocolate Walnut Fudge

3 cups sugar
3/4 cup (1 1/2 sticks) butter
1 (12-ounce) can evaporated milk
2 cups (12 ounces) semisweet chocolate chips
1 (7-ounce) jar marshmallow creme
1 teaspoon vanilla extract
1 cup chopped walnuts

Combine the sugar, butter and evaporated milk in a 3-quart heavy saucepan. Bring to a full rolling boil over medium heat, stirring constantly. Boil for 4 minutes, stirring constantly. Remove from the heat. Add the chocolate chips and marshmallow creme and stir until melted. Stir in the vanilla and walnuts. Spread in a foil-lined 9×9-inch pan. Cool at room temperature for at least 4 hours before cutting into squares.

Tammy Patterson, Lebanon

Fantasy Fudge

3 cups sugar
3/4 cup (1 1/2 sticks) butter
1 (5-ounce) can evaporated milk
12 ounces semisweet baking chocolate, chopped
1 (7-ounce) jar marshmallow creme
1 teaspoon vanilla extract

Combine the sugar, butter and evaporated milk in a 3-quart heavy saucepan. Bring to a full rolling boil over medium heat, stirring constantly. Cook for 4 minutes or to 234 degrees on a candy thermometer, soft-ball stage, stirring constantly. Remove from the heat. Add the chocolate and marshmallow creme and stir until melted. Stir in the vanilla. Spread immediately in a foil-lined 9×9-inch pan. Cool at room temperature for at least 4 hours before cutting into squares. Store in an airtight container.

Candy Nation, Lebanon

Miscellaneous Fudge

VANILLA FUDGE

1/2 cup (1 stick) margarine
1/2 cup milk
2 cups sugar
1 teaspoon vanilla extract

CHOCOLATE FUDGE

1/2 cup (1 stick) margarine
1/2 cup milk
3 tablespoons baking cocoa
2 cups sugar
1 teaspoon vanilla extract

For the vanilla fudge, melt the margarine in a saucepan over low heat. Add the milk and sugar and bring to a boil, stirring constantly. Remove from the heat. Add the vanilla and beat until smooth. Pour into a pan sprayed with nonstick cooking spray.

For the chocolate fudge, melt the margarine in a saucepan over low heat. Add the milk, baking cocoa and sugar and bring to a boil, stirring constantly. Remove from the heat. Add the vanilla and beat until smooth. Pour over the vanilla fudge layer. Cool completely before cutting into squares.

Mary Lou Ford, Lebanon

Devine Peanut Butter Fudge

Margarine for greasing
3/4 cup (1 1/2 sticks) margarine
3 cups sugar
2/3 cup evaporated milk
1 teaspoon vanilla extract
1 package peanut butter chips
1 (7-ounce) jar marshmallow creme
1 cup chopped nuts

Lightly grease an 8×12-inch pan with margarine. Bring 3/4 cup margarine, sugar and evaporated milk to a boil in a saucepan over high heat, stirring constantly. Reduce the heat to medium and cook for 5 minutes longer, stirring constantly. Remove from the heat and stir in the vanilla. Add the peanut butter chips and marshmallow creme and stir until melted and blended. Stir in the nuts. Pour into the prepared pan. Cool completely before cutting into squares.

Janet Devine, Mt. Juliet

Peanut Butter Chip Fudge

3/4 cup (1 1/2 sticks) margarine
3 cups sugar
1 (5-ounce) can evaporated milk
2 cups (12 ounces) peanut butter chips
1 (7-ounce) jar marshmallow creme
1 teaspoon vanilla extract

Microwave the margarine in a microwave-safe dish on High until mostly melted. Combine the melted margarine, sugar and evaporated milk in a lightly greased 4-quart saucepan. Bring to a full rolling boil over medium heat, stirring constantly. Continue to boil for 5 minutes. Remove from the heat. Stir in the peanut butter chips gradually until melted. Add the marshmallow creme and vanilla and mix well. Pour into a lightly greased pan. Cool completely before cutting into squares.

Russell Lane, Lebanon

Peanut Butter Fudge

3 cups sugar
3/4 cup milk
1/2 cup (1 stick) butter
1 cup creamy peanut butter or crunchy peanut butter
1 cup marshmallow creme
1 teaspoon vanilla extract

Combine the sugar, milk and butter in a saucepan and bring to a boil. Boil for 5 minutes, stirring constantly. Remove from the heat. Immediately add the peanut butter, marshmallow creme and vanilla and mix well. Pour into a buttered pan. Cool completely before cutting into squares.

Jenifer Hall, Mt. Juliet

Melt-In-Your-Mouth Peanut Butter Fudge

3 cups sugar
3/4 cup (1 1/2 sticks) margarine
2/3 cup evaporated milk
1 teaspoon vanilla extract
1 cup peanut butter
1 (7-ounce) jar marshmallow creme

Combine the sugar, margarine and evaporated milk in a heavy saucepan. Bring to a boil, stirring constantly. Boil for 4 minutes and remove from the heat. Immediately add the vanilla, peanut butter and marshmallow creme and stir until blended. Pour into a greased 9×13-inch pan. Cool completely before cutting into squares.

Julie Reynolds, Lebanon

Crunchy Peanut Butter Fudge

1 cup (2 sticks) butter
1 (1-pound) package light brown sugar
1/2 cup milk
3/4 cup crunchy peanut butter
1 (1-pound) package confectioners' sugar

Melt the butter in a saucepan. Stir in the brown sugar and milk. Bring to a boil and boil for 2 minutes, stirring constantly. Remove from the heat. Stir in the peanut butter. Add the confectioners' sugar and beat until smooth. Pour into a buttered dish. Cool completely before cutting into squares.

Dovie Marek, Lebanon

Yummy Peanut Butter Fudge

1/2 cup (1 stick) margarine
1 (12-ounce) can evaporated milk
4 cups sugar
1 (18-ounce) jar peanut butter
1 (7-ounce) jar marshmallow creme

Heat the margarine and evaporated milk in a large saucepan over medium heat until the margarine melts. Stir in the sugar. Cook for 11 minutes or to 234 to 240 degrees on a candy thermometer, soft-ball stage, stirring constantly. Remove from the heat. Add the peanut butter and marshmallow creme and stir until smooth. Pour into a greased 9×13-inch pan. Cool completely before cutting into squares.

Sue Singleton, Lebanon

Vanilla Chip Fudge

3/4 cup (1 1/2 sticks) margarine
3 cups sugar
1 (5-ounce) can evaporated milk
2 cups (12 ounces) vanilla chips
1 (7-ounce) jar marshmallow creme
1 teaspoon vanilla extract
1 cup chopped walnuts (optional)

Microwave the margarine in a microwave-safe dish on High until mostly melted. Combine the melted margarine, sugar and evaporated milk in a lightly greased 4-quart saucepan. Bring to a full rolling boil over medium heat, stirring constantly. Continue to boil for 5 minutes. Remove from the heat. Stir in the vanilla chips gradually until melted. Add the marshmallow creme and vanilla and mix well. Stir in the walnuts. Pour into a lightly greased pan. Cool completely before cutting into squares.

Russell Lane, Lebanon

Vanilla Pecan Fudge

3/4 cup (1 1/2 sticks) margarine
3 cups sugar
1 (5-ounce) can evaporated milk
1 package premium white chocolate chunks
1 (7-ounce) jar marshmallow creme
1 cup chopped pecans
1 tablespoon vanilla extract

Lightly butter a 9×13-inch or 9×9-inch pan. Combine the margarine, sugar and evaporated milk in a 2 1/2- to 3-quart heavy saucepan and mix well. Bring to a full rolling boil over medium heat, stirring constantly. Continue to boil for 5 minutes or to 234 degrees on a candy thermometer, soft-ball stage, stirring constantly. Remove from the heat. Stir in the white chocolate chunks gradually until melted. Add the marshmallow creme, pecans and vanilla and mix well. Pour into the prepared pan. Cool completely before cutting into squares.

Margaret Thompson Kilgore, Lebanon

Quick Vanilla Fudge

1/2 cup (1 stick) margarine
1/2 cup milk
2 cups sugar
1 teaspoon vanilla extract

Melt the margarine in a saucepan over low heat. Add the milk and sugar. Bring to a boil and boil for 2 minutes. Remove from the heat and beat until smooth. Stir in the vanilla. Pour into a pan sprayed with nonstick cooking spray. Cool completely before cutting into squares. You may add nuts, if desired.

Mary Lou Ford, Lebanon

Marshmallow Vanilla Fudge

3 cups sugar
3/4 cup (1 1/2 sticks) butter
1 (5-ounce) can evaporated milk
2 cups (12 ounces) vanilla chips
28 marshmallows
1 teaspoon vanilla extract
1 cup nuts

Mix the sugar, butter and evaporated milk in a heavy saucepan. Bring to a rolling boil and cook for 5 minutes, stirring constantly. Remove from the heat. Stir in the vanilla chips, marshmallows, vanilla and nuts. Pour into a greased pan. Cool completely before cutting into squares.

Irene Woodliff, Lebanon

White Chocolate Fudge

6 ounces white chocolate, grated
4 ounces cream cheese, softened
3 cups sifted confectioners' sugar
1/2 teaspoon vanilla extract
1 cup chopped pecans
Pecan halves
Melted white chocolate for drizzling

Melt 6 ounces white chocolate in a double boiler. Beat the cream cheese and confectioners' sugar at medium speed in a mixing bowl until smooth. Add the 6 ounces melted white chocolate and vanilla and beat well. Stir in the pecans. Press into a lightly greased 8×8-inch pan. Chill until firm and cut into squares. Top each square with a pecan half and drizzle with melted white chocolate.

Willette Piercey, Lebanon

Party Butter Mints

5 tablespoons butter
2 1/2 tablespoons evaporated milk
Few drops of mint extract
Food coloring
1 (1-pound) package confectioners' sugar

Melt the butter in a heavy saucepan. Stir in the evaporated milk and mint extract. Tint as desired with food coloring. Add the confectioners' sugar and mix well. Knead the mixture until smooth and press into candy molds. Unmold and let stand until desired firmness.

Judy Nosal, Lebanon

Cream Cheese Mints

3 ounces cream cheese, softened
1/2 teaspoon peppermint extract
3 cups sifted confectioners' sugar
Food coloring

Mix the cream cheese and peppermint extract in a bowl. Add the confectioners' sugar gradually, stirring constantly until smooth. Tint as desired with food coloring and knead until the food coloring is evenly distributed. Press about 3/4 teaspoon of the cream cheese mixture into each candy mold. Unmold and let stand, covered, at room temperature for 8 to 12 hours or until dry. Store, tightly covered, in the refrigerator.

Frances Baker, Lebanon

Cream Cheese Party Mints

3 ounces cream cheese, softened
1/2 teaspoon peppermint extract
3 cups sifted confectioners' sugar
Few drops of food coloring
Extra-fine granulated sugar

Combine the cream cheese and peppermint extract in a small mixing bowl and mix well. Add the confectioners' sugar gradually, beating until smooth and kneading in the last addition by hand. Knead in the food coloring until evenly distributed. Sprinkle small candy molds with granulated sugar. Press about 1/2 teaspoon of the mixture into the prepared candy molds. Unmold and let stand at room temperature for 8 to 12 hours or until dry.

Caryn Crowston, Mt. Juliet

Mints

3 ounces cream cheese, softened
3 cups sifted confectioners' sugar
1/2 teaspoon peppermint extract
Food coloring

Combine the cream cheese, confectioners' sugar and peppermint extract in a mixing bowl and beat until smooth and the desired consistency for molding. Tint with food coloring as desired. Press into candy molds. Unmold and let stand at room temperature for 8 to 12 hours or until dry.

Frances Baker, Lebanon

Peanut Brittle

2 cups sugar
1 cup light corn syrup
1/2 cup water
1/4 cup (1/2 stick) butter
4 cups raw peanuts
1 teaspoon baking soda

Combine the sugar, corn syrup, water and butter in a heavy saucepan and stir to mix. Cook to 230 degrees on a candy thermometer, spun-thread stage. Add the peanuts and cook to 280 degrees on a candy thermometer, soft-crack stage. Continue cooking to 305 degrees on a candy thermometer, hard-crack stage, stirring constantly. Remove from the heat. Add the baking soda, stirring constantly until the mixture foams. Pour immediately into 2 buttered 10×15-inch pans, spreading into a thin layer over the entire surface of the pans. Cool until firm and break into pieces.

Robin Nation, Lebanon

Cocktail Peanut Brittle

1/2 cup light corn syrup
1 cup sugar
1 1/2 cups cocktail peanuts
1 teaspoon baking soda

Combine the corn syrup and sugar in a 12-inch heavy skillet and stir to mix. Cook over high heat until the sugar melts. Add the peanuts. Cook until the syrup turns the color of the peanuts, stirring constantly. Remove from the heat and stir until the bubbles subside. Sprinkle with the baking soda and fold in. Pour into a buttered pan, moving the pan while pouring to cover the surface; do not spread. Cool until firm and break into small pieces from the backside.

Katherine Schubeck, Lebanon

Microwave Peanut Brittle

1 cup sugar
1/2 cup corn syrup
2 cups salted peanuts
1 tablespoon butter
1 teaspoon vanilla extract
1 teaspoon baking soda

Combine the sugar and corn syrup in a microwave-safe dish and mix well. Microwave on High for 5 minutes. Add the peanuts. Microwave for 3 1/2 minutes. Add the butter and vanilla. Microwave for 1 1/2 minutes longer or until the peanuts are light brown. Add the baking soda and stir until light and foamy. Pour on a lightly greased baking sheet. Let stand for 1 hour or until cool and break into pieces.

Patricia Bryant, Lebanon

Peanut Butter Crèmes

1 egg, well beaten
1/3 cup crunchy peanut butter or creamy peanut butter
1 tablespoon butter, softened
1/2 teaspoon vanilla extract
1/8 teaspoon salt
2 1/2 cups confectioners' sugar
Shredded coconut, granola or miniature chocolate chips

Combine the egg, peanut butter, butter, vanilla and salt in a bowl and mix well with a fork. Add the confectioners' sugar 1/2 cup at a time, mixing well with a fork after each addition and adding additional confectioners' sugar if needed for the desired consistency due to the variance caused by peanut butter brands. Shape the mixture into 1-inch balls and roll in coconut to coat. Place on a tray and chill until firm. You may also freeze, if desired. Note: If you are concerned about using raw eggs, use eggs pasteurized in their shells, which are sold at some specialty food stores, or use an equivalent amount of pasteurized egg substitute.

Alicia Hovies, Lebanon

Cookies

Jumbo Chocolate Chip Cookies

3/4 cup shortening
1 1/4 cups firmly packed light brown sugar
2 tablespoons milk
1 tablespoon vanilla extract
1 egg
1 3/4 cups all-purpose flour
1 teaspoon salt
3/4 teaspoon baking soda
1 1/2 cups (9 ounces) semisweet chocolate chips

Combine the shortening, brown sugar, milk and vanilla in a mixing bowl and beat at medium speed until blended. Beat in the egg. Combine the flour, salt and baking soda in a bowl. Add to the creamed mixture and mix just until blended. Stir in the chocolate chips. Drop by heaping tablespoonfuls 3 inches apart onto an ungreased cookie sheet. Bake at 375 degrees for 8 to 10 minutes or until light brown. Cool on the cookie sheet for 2 minutes. Remove to aluminum foil to cool completely.

Jan Fletcher, Lebanon

The Best Chocolate Chip Cookies

1/2 cup granulated sugar
1/2 cup packed brown sugar
1/3 cup butter, softened
1/3 cup shortening
1 egg
1 teaspoon vanilla extract
1 1/2 cups self-rising flour
1 cup (6 ounces) semisweet chocolate chips

Combine the granulated sugar, brown sugar, butter, shortening, egg and vanilla in a mixing bowl and beat until blended. Add the flour and mix well. Stir in the chocolate chips. Drop by rounded teaspoonfuls onto an ungreased cookie sheet. Bake at 375 degrees for 8 to 10 minutes or until light brown. Cool on the cookie sheet for 2 minutes. Remove to a wire rack to cool completely.

Leasa Gammon, Lebanon

Chocolate Chip Cookies

$^1/_2$ cup (1 stick) butter, softened
$^1/_2$ cup shortening
1 cup granulated sugar
$^1/_2$ cup packed brown sugar
2 eggs
2 cups plus 2 tablespoons all-purpose flour
1 teaspoon baking soda
1 teaspoon salt
1 teaspoon vanilla extract
1 cup (6 ounces) chocolate chips

Cream the butter and shortening in a mixing bowl. Add the granulated sugar, brown sugar and eggs and mix well. Combine the flour, baking soda and salt in a bowl. Add to the creamed mixture and mix well. Stir in the vanilla and chocolate chips. Drop by teaspoonfuls onto an ungreased cookie sheet. Bake at 350 degrees for 8 to 10 minutes or until the edges just turn golden brown. Cool on the cookie sheet for 2 minutes. Remove to a wire rack to cool completely.

Lynna Nix, Watertown

Chocolate Chipits Cookies

1 1/4 cups (2 1/2 sticks) butter, softened
1 cup granulated sugar
1 cup packed brown sugar
2 eggs
2 cups all-purpose flour
1 1/2 teaspoons baking soda
1/2 teaspoon salt
6 ounces Chipits chocolate baking chips

Cream the butter, granulated sugar and brown sugar in a mixing bowl until light and fluffy. Add the eggs and mix well. Combine the flour, baking soda and salt in a bowl. Add to the creamed mixture and mix well. Stir in the baking chips. Drop by spoonfuls onto a nonstick cookie sheet. Bake at 350 degrees for 8 to 10 minutes or until light brown. Cool on the cookie sheet for 2 minutes. Remove to a wire rack to cool completely.

Shelagh Mason, Watertown

Nutty Chocolate Chip Cookies

2/3 cup shortening
2/3 cup margarine, softened
1 cup granulated sugar
1 cup packed brown sugar
2 eggs
2 teaspoons vanilla extract
3 cups self-rising flour
2 cups (12 ounces) chocolate chips
1 cup chopped nuts

Cream the shortening, margarine, granulated sugar and brown sugar in a mixing bowl until light and fluffy. Add the eggs and vanilla and beat until blended. Add the flour and mix well by hand. Stir in the chocolate chips and nuts. Drop by teaspoonfuls 2 inches apart onto an ungreased cookie sheet. Bake at 325 degrees for 8 to 10 minutes or until light brown. Cool on the cookie sheet for 2 minutes. Remove to a wire rack to cool completely.

Kathleen Taylor, Watertown

No-Bake Cookies

1/2 cup (1 stick) margarine
2 cups sugar
1/2 cup milk
1/2 cup peanut butter
2 cups rolled oats

Melt the margarine in a saucepan. Add the sugar and milk. Bring to a boil and boil for 1 minute. Remove from the heat and add the peanut butter, stirring until melted. Add the oats and mix well. Drop by tablespoonfuls onto waxed paper. Let stand until cool. You may add 2 tablespoons baking cocoa with the sugar or add nuts, if desired.

Mary Lou Ford, Lebanon

No-Bake Chocolate Oatmeal Cookies

2 cups sugar
1/2 cup milk
1/2 cup (1 stick) butter or margarine
1/4 cup baking cocoa
1/2 cup peanut butter
3 cups quick-cooking oats

Combine the sugar, milk, butter and baking cocoa in a saucepan. Bring to a boil and boil for 1 minute. Remove from the heat. Add the peanut butter and oats and mix well. Drop by tablespoonfuls onto waxed paper. Let stand until cool.

Stacy Reeves, Watertown

Oatmeal Cookies

1 cup butter-flavored shortening
1 cup granulated sugar
1/2 cup firmly packed light brown sugar
2 eggs
2 teaspoons vanilla extract
2 cups all-purpose flour
1 teaspoon baking soda
1 teaspoon salt
1 cup quick-cooking oats

Cream the shortening, granulated sugar and brown sugar in a mixing bowl until light and fluffy. Add the eggs and vanilla and beat at medium speed until blended. Combine the flour, baking soda and salt in a bowl. Add to the creamed mixture gradually, beating constantly at low speed. Stir in the oats. Drop by teaspoonfuls 2 inches apart onto a greased cookie sheet. Bake at 375 degrees for 10 to 12 minutes or until light brown. Cool on the cookie sheet for 2 minutes. Remove to a wire rack to cool completely.

Candy Nation, Lebanon

Oatmeal Cinnamon Cookies

3/4 cup (1 1/2 sticks) butter, softened
1 cup packed brown sugar
1/2 cup granulated sugar
1/2 teaspoon ground cinnamon
1 teaspoon baking powder
1/4 teaspoon baking soda
2 eggs
1 teaspoon vanilla extract
1 3/4 cups all-purpose flour
2 cups rolled oats

Beat the butter at medium speed in a mixing bowl for 30 seconds. Add the brown sugar, granulated sugar, cinnamon, baking powder and baking soda and beat until blended, stopping to scrape the side of the bowl occasionally. Beat in the eggs and vanilla. Add the flour and mix well. Stir in the oats. Drop by rounded teaspoonfuls 2 inches apart on an ungreased cookie sheet. Bake at 375 degrees for 8 to 10 minutes or until light brown. Cool on the cookie sheet for 2 minutes. Remove to a wire rack to cool completely.

Robin Nation, Lebanon

Spiced Oatmeal Cookies

1 1/2 cups all-purpose flour
1/2 teaspoon salt
1 teaspoon baking soda
1 teaspoon ground cinnamon
1/2 teaspoon ground cloves
1 cup (2 sticks) butter, softened
1 cup packed light brown sugar
1/2 cup granulated sugar
2 eggs
1 teaspoon vanilla extract
3 cups rolled oats

Combine the flour, salt, baking soda, cinnamon and cloves in a bowl. Cream the butter, brown sugar and granulated sugar in a mixing bowl until light and fluffy. Add the eggs and vanilla and beat until blended. Add the flour mixture gradually, beating constantly until blended. Stir in the oats. Drop by heaping tablespoonfuls 2 inches apart onto an ungreased cookie sheet. Bake at 325 degrees for 12 minutes or until golden brown. Cool on the cookie sheet for 2 minutes. Remove to a wire rack to cool completely.

Karen Smith, Lebanon

Coconut Oatmeal Cookies

2 cups all-purpose flour
1 teaspoon baking powder
1 teaspoon baking soda
1 teaspoon salt
1 cup (2 sticks) butter or margarine, softened
1 cup packed brown sugar
1 cup granulated sugar
2 eggs
1 teaspoon vanilla extract
2 cups rolled oats
2 cups flaked coconut

Sift together the first 4 ingredients. Cream the butter in a mixing bowl. Beat in the brown sugar and granulated sugar until light and fluffy. Blend in the eggs and vanilla. Mix in the flour mixture. Stir in the oats and coconut. Drop by spoonfuls onto a nonstick cookie sheet. Bake at 350 degrees for 7 to 9 minutes or just until the edges begin to brown. Cool on the cookie sheet for 1 minute. Remove to aluminum foil to cool completely.

Karen Oldham Franklin, Mt. Juliet

Oatmeal Raisin Cookies

1 cup (2 sticks) butter, softened
1 cup packed brown sugar
1/2 cup granulated sugar
2 eggs
1 teaspoon vanilla extract
1 3/4 cups self-rising flour
1 teaspoon ground cinnamon
4 cups rolled oats
1 cup raisins

Cream the butter, brown sugar and granulated sugar in a mixing bowl until light and fluffy. Blend in the eggs and vanilla. Beat in the flour and cinnamon gradually until blended. Stir in the oats and raisins. Drop by spoonfuls onto a nonstick cookie sheet. Bake at 350 degrees for 10 minutes. Cool on the cookie sheet for 2 minutes. Remove to a wire rack to cool completely.

Kathy Settle, Lebanon

Oatmeal Toffee Cookies

1 cup (2 sticks) butter, softened
2 cups packed light brown sugar
2 eggs, beaten
2 teaspoons vanilla extract
1 3/4 cups all-purpose flour
1 teaspoon baking soda
1 teaspoon ground cinnamon
1/2 teaspoon salt
3 cups rolled oats
1 (8-ounce) package almond toffee bits
1 cup sweetened coconut flakes (optional)

Combine the butter, brown sugar, eggs and vanilla in a large mixing bowl and beat until blended. Add the flour, baking soda, cinnamon and salt and mix well. Stir in the oats, toffee bits and coconut. Drop by cookie scoopfuls 2 inches apart onto a nonstick cookie sheet. Bake at 375 degrees for 10 to 12 minutes or until light brown. Cool on the cookie sheet for 2 minutes. Remove to a wire rack to cool completely.

Rachel Gregory, Lebanon

Peanut Butter Cookies

1/2 cup (1 stick) butter or margarine, softened
1/2 cup peanut butter
1 cup sugar
2 eggs
1/2 teaspoon vanilla extract
1 cup all-purpose flour
1 teaspoon baking powder
1 teaspoon salt

Cream the butter, peanut butter and sugar in a mixing bowl. Beat in the eggs 1 at a time. Stir in the vanilla. Combine the flour, baking powder and salt in a bowl. Stir into the peanut butter mixture. Drop by rounded spoonfuls 2 inches apart onto an ungreased cookie sheet. Bake at 350 degrees for 8 to 10 minutes or until light brown. Press the back of a fork onto the hot cookies in a crisscross pattern. Cool completely on the cookie sheet.

Lynna Nix, Watertown

Robin's Peanut Butter Cookies

1/2 cup (1 stick) butter, softened
1/2 cup peanut butter
1/2 cup granulated sugar
1/2 cup packed brown sugar
1/2 teaspoon baking powder
1/2 teaspoon baking soda
1 egg
1/2 teaspoon vanilla extract
1 1/4 cups all-purpose flour
Granulated sugar for coating

Combine the butter and peanut butter in a mixing bowl and beat at medium to high speed for 30 seconds. Add 1/2 cup granulated sugar, the brown sugar, baking powder and baking soda and beat until blended. Beat in the egg and vanilla. Add the flour and mix well. Chill for 30 minutes. Shape into 1-inch balls. Roll in additional granulated sugar to coat. Place 2 inches apart onto an ungreased cookie sheet. Press the back of a fork into the dough in a crisscross pattern. Bake at 375 degrees for 7 to 9 minutes or until light brown. Cool on the cookie sheet for 2 minutes. Remove to a wire rack to cool completely.

Robin Nation, Lebanon

Easy Peanut Butter Cookies

1/2 cup shortening
1/2 cup peanut butter
1/2 cup granulated sugar
1/2 cup packed brown sugar
1 egg
1 1/4 cups self-rising flour

Combine the shortening and peanut butter in a mixing bowl and beat until blended. Add the granulated sugar and brown sugar and beat until blended. Beat in the egg. Add the flour and mix well. Shape into 1-inch balls. Place 2 inches apart on a nonstick cookie sheet. Press the back of a fork into the dough in a crisscross pattern. Bake at 375 degrees for 10 minutes. Cool on the cookie sheet for 2 minutes. Remove to a wire rack to cool completely.

Mary Lou Ford, Lebanon

Creamy Peanut Butter Cookies

3/4 cup creamy peanut butter
1/2 cup shortening
1 1/4 cups packed light brown sugar
3 tablespoons milk
1 teaspoon vanilla extract
1 egg
1 3/4 cups all-purpose flour
3/4 teaspoon baking soda
3/4 teaspoon salt

Combine the peanut butter, shortening, brown sugar, milk and vanilla in a mixing bowl and beat until blended. Beat in the egg. Add the flour, baking soda and salt and mix well. Drop by tablespoonfuls onto an ungreased cookie sheet. Press the back of a fork into the dough in a crisscross pattern. Bake at 375 degrees for 7 to 9 minutes or until light brown. Cool on the cookie sheet for 2 minutes. Remove to a wire rack to cool completely.

Robin Nation, Lebanon

Corky's Snickerdoodles

1 cup (2 sticks) margarine, softened
1½ cups sugar
2 eggs
2¾ cups all-purpose flour
2 teaspoons cream of tartar
1 teaspoon baking soda
¼ teaspoon salt
¼ cup pecan meal
2 tablespoons sugar
2 teaspoons ground cinnamon

Combine the margarine, 1½ cups sugar and the eggs in a mixing bowl and beat until blended. Combine the flour, cream of tartar, baking soda and salt in a bowl. Add to the egg mixture and mix well. Stir in the pecan meal. Shape into 1-inch balls. Combine 2 tablespoons sugar and the cinnamon in a shallow dish. Roll the dough balls in the cinnamon mixture to coat. Place 2 inches apart on an ungreased cookie sheet. Bake at 400 degrees for 8 to 10 minutes or until light brown. Cool on the cookie sheet for 2 minutes. Remove to a wire rack to cool completely.

Corky Sharpe, Mt. Juliet

The Best Snickerdoodles

1/2 cup (1 stick) butter or margarine, softened
1/2 cup shortening
1 1/2 cups sugar
2 eggs
2 1/4 cups all-purpose flour
2 teaspoons cream of tartar
1 teaspoon baking soda
1/4 teaspoon salt
2 tablespoons sugar
2 teaspoons ground cinnamon

Combine the butter, shortening, 1 1/2 cups sugar and the eggs in a mixing bowl and beat until blended. Combine the flour, cream of tartar, baking soda and salt in a bowl. Add to the egg mixture and mix well. Shape by rounded teaspoonfuls into balls. Combine 2 tablespoons sugar and the cinnamon in a shallow dish. Roll the dough balls in the cinnamon mixture to coat. Place 2 inches apart on an ungreased cookie sheet. Bake at 400 degrees for 8 to 10 minutes or until light brown. Remove to a wire rack immediately to cool.

Alicia Hovies, Lebanon

Brown Sugar Snickerdoodles

1/2 cup (1 stick) butter, softened
1/2 cup shortening
2 eggs
1 cup granulated sugar
1/2 cup packed brown sugar
2 cups plus 2 tablespoons all-purpose flour
1 teaspoon baking soda
1 teaspoon salt
1 teaspoon vanilla extract
2 tablespoons ground cinnamon
6 tablespoons granulated sugar

Combine the butter, shortening, eggs, 1 cup granulated sugar and the brown sugar in a mixing bowl and beat until blended. Add the flour, baking soda and salt and mix well. Stir in the vanilla. Drop by teaspoonfuls 3 inches apart onto a nonstick cookie sheet. Bake at 350 degrees for 8 to 10 minutes or until light brown. Combine the cinnamon and 6 tablespoons granulated sugar in a small bowl. Sprinkle on the hot cookies. Remove the cookies to a wire rack to cool completely.

Lynna Nix, Lebanon

Snickerdoodles

$2^3/4$ cups all-purpose flour
1 teaspoon cream of tartar
1 teaspoon baking soda
$^1/4$ teaspoon salt
$^1/2$ cup shortening
$^1/2$ cup (1 stick) margarine, softened
$1^1/2$ cups sugar
2 eggs
1 teaspoon vanilla extract
2 tablespoons sugar
2 teaspoons ground cinnamon

Combine the flour, cream of tartar, baking soda and salt in a bowl. Combine the shortening, margarine, $1^1/2$ cups sugar and the eggs in a mixing bowl and beat until blended. Add the flour mixture and mix well. Stir in the vanilla. Shape into 1-inch balls. Combine 2 tablespoons sugar and the cinnamon in a shallow dish. Roll the dough balls in the cinnamon mixture to coat. Place 2 inches apart onto an ungreased cookie sheet. Bake at 400 degrees for 8 to 10 minutes or until the cookies puff up and flatten out. Reduce the oven temperature to 350 degrees. Bake for 15 to 20 minutes or until light brown. Remove to a wire rack to cool completely.

Margaret Thompson Kilgore, Lebanon

Sugar Cookies

1 cup (2 sticks) margarine, softened
2 cups sugar
2 eggs
1/2 cup milk
1 1/2 teaspoons vanilla extract
5 cups sifted self-rising flour

Combine the margarine, sugar, eggs, milk and vanilla in a mixing bowl and beat until blended. Add the flour and mix well. Roll to 1/8 inch on a floured surface. Cut as desired and place on a nonstick cookie sheet. Bake at 350 degrees for 10 minutes. Cool on the cookie sheet for 2 minutes. Remove to a wire rack to cool completely.

Mary Lou Ford, Lebanon

Old-Fashioned Sugar Cookies

3 1/2 cups sifted all-purpose flour
2 1/2 teaspoons baking powder
1/2 teaspoon salt
1 cup (2 sticks) butter or margarine, softened
1 1/2 cups sugar
2 eggs
3 teaspoons vanilla extract
Sugar

Sift together the flour, baking powder and salt. Beat the butter, 1 1/2 cups sugar, the eggs and vanilla in a bowl until light and fluffy. Add the flour mixture gradually, blending well after each addition. Chill the dough for 30 minutes. Shape the dough into 1-inch balls. Place on a nonstick cookie sheet. Flatten to about 1/8 inch with a glass dipped in additional sugar. Bake at 400 degrees for 10 to 12 minutes or until the edges are golden brown. Remove to a wire rack to cool completely.

Frances Baker, Lebanon

Kathy's Sugar Cookies

2/3 cup shortening
3/4 cup sugar
1 egg
1 teaspoon vanilla extract
4 teaspoons milk
2 cups all-purpose flour
1 1/2 teaspoons baking powder
1/4 teaspoon salt

Cream the shortening in a mixing bowl. Add the sugar, egg and vanilla and beat until light and fluffy. Add the milk, flour, baking powder and salt and mix well. Place on a floured surface and knead 15 times. Divide the dough into halves. Sprinkle each half with flour and chill, wrapped in plastic wrap, for 24 hours. Roll dough 1/8 inch thick on a floured surface. Cut as desired and place on a nonstick cookie sheet. Sprinkle with sugar. Bake at 375 degrees for 8 minutes. Cool on the cookie sheet for 2 minutes. Remove to a wire rack to cool completely.

Kathy Settle, Lebanon

Sugar Cookie Cutouts

2/3 cup butter, softened
3/4 cup sugar
1 teaspoon baking powder
1/4 teaspoon salt
1 egg
1 tablespoon milk
1 teaspoon vanilla extract
2 cups all-purpose flour

Beat the butter in a mixing bowl until creamy. Add the sugar, baking powder and salt and beat until blended. Beat in the egg, milk and vanilla. Add the flour and mix well. Divide the dough into halves. Chill, wrapped in plastic wrap, for 30 minutes or until easy to handle. Roll dough 1/8 inch thick on a floured surface. Cut as desired and place 1 inch apart on an ungreased cookie sheet. Bake at 375 degrees for 7 to 8 minutes or until light brown. Remove to a wire rack to cool completely. Decorate as desired.

Robin Nation, Lebanon

Confectioners' Sugar Cookies

5 cups all-purpose flour
1 teaspoon baking soda
1 teaspoon cream of tartar
1 teaspoon salt
1 cup confectioners' sugar
1 cup granulated sugar
1 cup (2 sticks) margarine, softened
1 cup vegetable oil
2 eggs
2 teaspoons vanilla extract
Granulated sugar

Sift together the flour, baking soda, cream of tartar and salt. Cream the confectioners' sugar, granulated sugar, margarine and oil in a mixing bowl until light and fluffy. Beat in the eggs and vanilla. Add the flour mixture and mix well. Shape into balls and place on an ungreased cookie sheet. Flatten with a glass dipped in additional granulated sugar. You may also press through a cookie press onto an ungreased cookie sheet. Bake at 350 degrees for 15 to 20 minutes or until light brown. Remove to a wire rack to cool completely.

Margaret Thompson Kilgore, Lebanon

Iced Sugar Cookies

4 cups all-purpose flour
2 1/2 teaspoons baking powder
1/2 teaspoon salt
2/3 cup shortening
1 1/2 cups granulated sugar
2 eggs
1 teaspoon vanilla extract
4 teaspoons milk
Confectioners' sugar
Water

Sift together the flour, baking powder and salt. Cream the shortening, granulated sugar, eggs and vanilla in a mixing bowl until light and fluffy. Add the flour mixture alternately with the milk, mixing well after each addition. Chill, wrapped in plastic wrap, in the refrigerator. Roll half the dough 1/8 inch thick on a floured surface. Cut as desired and place on a nonstick cookie sheet. Bake at 350 degrees for 9 minutes. Cool on the cookie sheet for 2 minutes. Remove to a wire rack to cool completely. Combine enough confectioners' sugar and water in a bowl to reach the desired spreading consistency. Spread over the cooled cookies.

Betty Ricketts, Lebanon

Cappuccino Toffee Cookies

1/2 cup (1 stick) butter, softened
1/2 cup shortening
1 cup granulated sugar
1/2 cup packed brown sugar
2 eggs
2 cups plus 2 tablespoons all-purpose flour
1 teaspoon baking soda
1 teaspoon salt
1 teaspoon vanilla extract
1/4 cup Folgers Café Latte Mocha Fusion Mix
2 tablespoons hot water
1 toffee candy bar, crushed

Cream the butter and shortening in a mixing bowl. Add the granulated sugar and brown sugar and beat until light and fluffy. Add the eggs, flour, baking soda, salt and vanilla and mix well. Combine the mocha fusion mix and water in a small bowl and stir until the mix is dissolved. Add to the cookie dough and mix well. Stir in the crushed candy bar. Drop by teaspoonfuls onto an ungreased cookie sheet. Bake at 350 degrees for 8 to 10 minutes or until the edges just begin to turn golden. Cool on the cookie sheet for 2 minutes. Remove to a wire rack to cool completely.

Lynna Nix, Watertown

Lemon Tea Cookies

1/2 cup milk
2 teaspoons lemon juice
2 cups all-purpose flour
1 teaspoon baking soda
1/4 teaspoon salt
1/2 cup (1 stick) butter, softened
3/4 cup sugar
1 egg
1 teaspoon finely shredded lemon zest
3/4 cup sugar
1/4 cup lemon juice

Stir together the milk and 2 teaspoons lemon juice in a small bowl. Combine the flour, baking soda and salt in a bowl. Cream the butter in a large mixing bowl. Add 3/4 cup sugar and beat until light and fluffy. Add the egg and lemon zest and beat well. Add the flour mixture and milk mixture alternately, beating well after each addition. Drop by a level cookie scoop onto an ungreased cookie sheet. Bake at 350 degrees for 12 to 14 minutes or until golden brown. Stir together 3/4 cup sugar and 1/4 cup lemon juice in a small bowl. Brush on the hot cookies.

Rachel Gregory, Lebanon

Brownies

1/2 cup (1 stick) margarine, softened
1 cup sugar
2 eggs
3/4 cup all-purpose flour
1/4 cup baking cocoa
2 teaspoons baking soda
2 teaspoons salt
1 teaspoon cream of tartar
1/2 teaspoon vanilla extract

Cream the margarine and sugar in a mixing bowl. Add the eggs and beat until blended. Add the flour, baking cocoa, baking soda, salt, cream of tartar and vanilla and mix well. Pour into a square baking pan. Bake at 350 degrees for 35 to 40 minutes or until the brownies test done.

Tammy Patterson, Lebanon

Walnut Brownies

1 cup (2 sticks) butter, softened
2 cups sugar
2 teaspoons vanilla extract
4 eggs
1 cup all-purpose flour
5 to 6 tablespoons baking cocoa
2 cups chopped walnuts

Cream the butter, sugar and vanilla in a mixing bowl. Add the eggs and beat until blended. Add the flour and baking cocoa and mix well. Stir in the walnuts. Pour into a greased 9×13-inch baking pan. Bake at 350 degrees for 35 minutes.

Kathy Settle, Lebanon

Favorite Brownies

3/4 cup baking cocoa
1/4 cup shortening
1 cup (2 sticks) butter
4 eggs, beaten
2 cups sugar
1 teaspoon vanilla extract
1 cup all-purpose flour
1/4 teaspoon salt
1 to 2 cups chopped nuts (optional)

Heat the baking cocoa, shortening and butter in a saucepan until the shortening and butter are melted. Pour into a mixing bowl and let stand until cool. Add the eggs and sugar and beat until the mixture is thickened. Add the vanilla and mix well. Add the flour and salt and beat until blended. Stir in the nuts. Pour into a greased 9×13-inch baking pan. Bake at 350 degrees for 25 to 30 minutes or until the middle of the cake is of a fudge consistency and the top is shiny and firm. Cool completely before cutting.

Alicia Hovies, Lebanon

Nutty Chocolate Chip Brownies

5 ounces dark chocolate, finely chopped
1/2 cup sunflower oil
1 1/4 cups packed light brown sugar
2 eggs
1 teaspoon vanilla extract
1/2 cup self-rising flour
1/4 cup baking cocoa
1/4 cup walnuts or pecans, chopped
1/4 cup milk chocolate chips

Melt the dark chocolate in a heatproof bowl set over a saucepan of barely simmering water. Combine the sunflower oil, brown sugar, eggs and vanilla in a large mixing bowl and beat until blended. Stir in the melted chocolate and beat until smooth. Sift the flour and baking cocoa into the bowl and fold into the mixture. Stir in the walnuts and chocolate chips. Pour into a lightly greased 8×8-inch shallow baking pan. Bake at 350 degrees for 30 to 35 minutes or until the top is firm and crusty.

Jan Rich, Mt. Juliet

Raspberry Truffle Brownies

3/4 cup (1 1/2 sticks) unsalted butter
4 ounces unsweetened chocolate, chopped
3 eggs
2 cups granulated sugar
1/3 cup raspberry jam
3 tablespoons black raspberry liqueur such as Chambord or other berry liqueur
1 cup all-purpose flour
1/4 teaspoon salt
1 cup (6 ounces) semisweet chocolate chips
Confectioners' sugar

Melt the butter and unsweetened chocolate in a large saucepan over low heat, stirring until smooth and blended. Remove from the heat. Whisk in the eggs, granulated sugar, jam and liqueur. Add the flour and salt and mix well. Stir in the chocolate chips. Pour into a 9-inch springform pan sprayed with nonstick cooking spray. Bake at 350 degrees for 45 minutes or until a wooden pick inserted in the center comes out with moist crumbs attached. Cool in the pan on a wire rack. Run a knife around the rim of the pan. Remove the side of the pan. Dust with confectioners' sugar. Cut into wedges and serve. You may prepare the brownies up to 2 days in advance. Store, wrapped tightly in plastic wrap, at room temperature.

June Thomas, Lebanon

Cherry Cheese Bars

3/4 cup (1 1/2 sticks) butter or margarine, softened
3/4 cup sugar
1 egg
1 1/2 cups all-purpose flour
1/4 teaspoon salt
2 to 4 tablespoons all-purpose flour
8 ounces cream cheese, softened
1 egg
1 cup cherry preserves

Cream the butter and sugar in a large mixing bowl until light and fluffy. Add 1 egg and beat until blended. Stir in 1 1/2 cups flour and the salt. Reserve 1 cup of the mixture. Press the remaining mixture into a greased 9×13-inch baking pan. Bake at 350 degrees for 15 minutes.

Combine 2 to 4 tablespoons flour with the reserved mixture in a bowl and mix until crumbly. Beat the cream cheese and 1 egg in a mixing bowl until blended. Spread the cream cheese mixture over the baked layer. Spread the preserves over the cream cheese layer. Sprinkle with the crumb mixture. Bake at 350 degrees for 35 to 40 minutes or until the edge is golden brown. Let cool completely.

June Thomas, Lebanon

Crème de Menthe Bars

COOKIE BARS
1 cup (2 sticks) butter, softened
1 cup sugar
4 eggs
1 cup all-purpose flour
1/2 teaspoon salt
1 (16-ounce) can chocolate syrup
1 tablespoon vanilla extract

CRÈME DE MENTHE FROSTING
2 cups confectioners' sugar
1/2 cup (1 stick) butter, softened
1/4 cup crème de menthe liqueur

CHOCOLATE TOPPING
1 cup (6 ounces) semisweet chocolate chips
6 tablespoons butter

For the bars, beat the butter and sugar in a mixing bowl until light and fluffy. Add the eggs 1 at a time, beating well after each addition. Stir in the flour, salt, chocolate syrup and vanilla. Pour into a greased 9×13-inch baking pan. Bake at 350 degrees for 30 minutes. Let stand until cool.

For the frosting, combine the confectioners' sugar, butter and liqueur in a mixing bowl and beat until blended. Spread over the cooled bars. Refrigerate until set.

For the topping, melt the chocolate chips and butter in a saucepan, stirring until blended. Spread over the frosting layer.

Lynna Nix, Watertown

Lemon Bars

1 cup all-purpose flour
1/2 cup confectioners' sugar
1/2 cup (1 stick) butter
2 eggs
1 cup granulated sugar
1/4 teaspoon salt
1/4 teaspoon grated lemon zest
2 tablespoons lemon juice
3 ounces cream cheese, softened
1 tablespoon confectioners' sugar

Combine the flour and 1/2 cup confectioners' sugar in a bowl. Cut in the butter until crumbly. Press in the bottom of an 8×8-inch baking pan. Bake at 350 degrees for 15 minutes.

Beat the eggs, granulated sugar and salt in a mixing bowl until fluffy. Add the lemon zest and lemon juice and mix well. Add the cream cheese and beat until blended. Pour over the baked layer. Bake at 350 degrees for 25 minutes. Let cool completely. Sift 1 tablespoon confectioners' sugar over the top.

Angela Collom, Watertown

Pecan Squares

2 cups all-purpose flour
2/3 cup confectioners' sugar
3/4 cup (1 1/2 sticks) butter, softened
1/2 cup firmly packed brown sugar
1/2 cup honey
2/3 cup butter
3 tablespoons heavy cream or whipping cream
3 1/2 cups coarsely chopped pecans

Sift together the flour and confectioners' sugar into a bowl. Cut in 3/4 cup butter with a pastry knife or a fork just until the mixture resembles coarse crumbs. Press over the bottom and 1 1/2 inches up the sides of a lightly greased 9×13-inch baking pan. Bake at 350 degrees for 20 minutes or until the edges are light brown.

Combine the brown sugar, honey, 2/3 cup butter and cream in a saucepan and bring to a boil over medium-high heat. Stir in the pecans. Pour the hot filling into the cooled crust. Bake at 350 degrees for 25 to 30 minutes or until golden brown and bubbly. Cool completely before cutting into squares.

Amy Upchurch, Watertown

Toffee Cookie Bars

1/2 cup (1 stick) butter or margarine
1 1/2 cups graham cracker crumbs
1 (14-ounce) can sweetened condensed milk
1 1/4 cups almond toffee bits
1 1/4 cups English toffee bits
1 cup (6 ounces) semisweet chocolate chips
1 cup chopped pecans
1/2 cup sliced almonds

Place the butter in a 9×13-inch baking pan. Heat in a 325-degree oven for 4 minutes or until melted. Sprinkle with the graham cracker crumbs. Pour the sweetened condensed milk over the crumb layer. Sprinkle with the toffee bits, chocolate chips, pecans and almonds. Press the layers lightly. Bake at 325 degrees for 25 minutes or until the edges are light brown. Cool completely on a wire rack before cutting into bars.

Amy Upchurch, Watertown

Pies

Apple Pie

PASTRY

3 cups all-purpose flour
1/2 teaspoon salt
3/4 cup shortening
1 to 2 teaspoons ice water

PIE

7 good-size apples, sliced
1 cup granulated sugar
1/4 cup packed brown sugar
1 tablespoon ground cinnamon
1/4 teaspoon ground cloves
Several pats of margarine
1 egg white
1/2 cup water

For the pastry, mix the flour and salt in a bowl. Cut in the shortening with a pastry blender until crumbly. Add the ice water a small amount at a time, mixing with a fork until the mixture forms a ball. Cover with plastic wrap and chill for 1 hour or longer. Roll the pastry into a circle on a floured surface. Fit into an ungreased pie plate, trimming and fluting the edge.

For the pie, combine the apples, granulated sugar, brown sugar, cinnamon and cloves in a bowl and toss to coat. Spoon into the prepared pie plate. Cover the apple mixture with the margarine. Brush with a mixture of the egg white and water. Bake at 375 degrees for 40 to 50 minutes or until bubbly.

Willette Piercey, Lebanon

Rachel's Apple Pie

PIE PASTRY
2 cups sifted all-purpose flour
1 teaspoon salt
3/4 cup shortening
4 to 5 tablespoons cold water

PIE
2/3 cup sugar
1 tablespoon all-purpose flour, sifted
4 cups thinly sliced Granny Smith apples
1/2 cup orange juice
3 tablespoons butter
1 teaspoon apple pie spice
Milk, or 1 egg white, lightly beaten

For the pastry, mix the flour and salt in a mixing bowl. Cut in the shortening with a pastry blender until the mixture is the consistency of coarse cornmeal or tiny peas. Sprinkle with cold water and mix lightly with a fork. Shape into a smooth flattened disk and wrap in plastic wrap. Chill for 30 minutes or longer.

For the pie, mix the sugar and flour in a bowl. Cook the apples in the orange juice in a saucepan until tender. Divide the pastry into 2 equal portions. Roll 1 portion into a circle on a floured surface. Fit into a pie plate, trimming and fluting the edge. Roll the remaining portion into a circle and cut into strips.

Pour the apple mixture into the prepared pie plate. Sprinkle with the sugar mixture. Dot with the butter and sprinkle with the apple pie spice. Arrange the pastry strips lattice-fashion over the pie and brush with milk. Bake at 375 degrees for 45 minutes.

Rachel Gregory, Lebanon

Lattice-Crust Apple Pie

PASTRY

2 1/3 cups all-purpose flour, sifted
1 tablespoon sugar
1/2 teaspoon ground cinnamon
1/4 teaspoon salt
1/2 cup (1 stick) butter, chilled and cut into small pieces
1/4 cup shortening
6 tablespoons cold water

PIE

7 Granny Smith apples, peeled, cored and thinly sliced
1/2 cup sugar
1 teaspoon ground cinnamon
1/4 teaspoon ground nutmeg
2 tablespoons butter, cut into small pieces
1 egg, lightly beaten

For the pastry, mix the flour, sugar, cinnamon and salt in a large bowl. Cut in the butter and shortening with a pastry blender or 2 knives until crumbly. Add the water 1 tablespoon at a time, mixing with a fork to form a dough. Divide the pastry into 2 equal portions and shape each portion into a disk. Wrap in plastic wrap and chill for 1 hour.

For the pie, combine the apples, sugar, cinnamon and nutmeg in a large bowl and toss to coat. Roll 1 portion of the pastry into an 11-inch circle on a lightly floured surface. Fit into a 9-inch pie plate. Spoon the apple mixture into the prepared pie plate and dot with the butter. Roll the remaining dough into a 10-inch circle on a lightly floured surface and cut into 1/2-inch strips. Arrange 2 strips in a cross pattern in the center of the pie, with the ends of the strips overlapping the bottom pastry. Alternately weave the remaining strips into a lattice pattern until the filling is covered. Brush with the egg. Bake at 400 degrees on the lowest oven rack for 40 minutes or until the pastry is golden brown and the filling is bubbly.

Laura S. Doucette, Mt. Juliet

Apple Crumb Pie

3 large Gala apples, peeled and thinly sliced
1 unbaked (9-inch) pie shell
1/2 cup sugar
1 teaspoon ground cinnamon
3/4 cup all-purpose flour
1/2 cup sugar
1/3 cup butter or margarine

Place the apples in the pie shell. Sprinkle with a mixture of 1/2 cup sugar and the cinnamon. Mix the flour and 1/2 cup sugar in a bowl. Cut in the butter until crumbly. Sprinkle over the top of the pie. Bake at 400 degrees for 40 minutes or until the top of the pie is a deep golden brown.

Leasa Gammon, Lebanon

Apple Praline Pie

1 (2-crust) pie pastry
1 cup granulated sugar
1/3 cup all-purpose flour
1 teaspoon ground cinnamon
8 cups thinly sliced peeled cooking apples
3 tablespoons butter
1/2 cup packed brown sugar
2 tablespoons half-and-half, light cream or milk
1/2 cup chopped pecans

Roll 1/2 of the pastry into a 12-inch circle on a lightly floured surface. Fit into a pie plate. Mix the granulated sugar, flour and cinnamon in a very large bowl. Add the apple slices and toss gently until well coated. Mound the apple slices into the prepared pie plate. Roll the remaining pastry into a 12-inch circle on a lightly floured surface. Place over the top of the pie, trimming and fluting the edge and cutting vents. Bake at 350 degrees for 35 minutes.

Combine the butter, brown sugar and half-and-half in a small saucepan and mix well. Bring to a boil and remove from the heat. Stir in the pecans. Remove the pie from the oven and place on a baking pan. Pour the brown sugar mixture over the hot pie. Return to the oven and bake for 5 minutes. Cool on a wire rack.

June Thomas, Lebanon

Double-Good Blueberry Pie

3/4 cup sugar
3 tablespoons cornstarch
1/8 teaspoon salt
1/4 cup water
4 cups blueberries
1 tablespoon butter
1 tablespoon lemon juice
1 baked (9-inch) pie shell

Mix the sugar, cornstarch and salt in a saucepan. Add the water and 2 cups of the blueberries. Cook over medium heat until the mixture comes to a boil and is thickened, stirring constantly. Remove from the heat and stir in the butter and lemon juice. Let stand until cool. Place the remaining 2 cups blueberries in the pie shell. Pour the cooked blueberry mixture over the top. Chill in the refrigerator. Serve with whipped topping or vanilla ice cream, or garnish with pastry cut outs.

Rachel Gregory, Lebanon

Chilled Blueberry Pie

Pecan halves
1 unbaked (9-inch) pie shell
8 ounces cream cheese, softened
2 cups confectioners' sugar
16 ounces whipped topping
1 (21-ounce) can blueberry pie filling

Press pecan halves into the bottom of the pie shell. Bake at 450 degrees for 10 to 12 minutes or until golden brown. Remove from the oven and let stand until cool.

Process the cream cheese and confectioners' sugar in a blender until smooth. Pour into the cooled crust. Spread 1/2 of the whipped topping over the cream cheese layer. Spread the pie filling over the whipped topping layer. Top with the remaining whipped topping. Chill in the refrigerator.

June Thomas, Lebanon

Stars and Stripes Pie

2 (15-ounce) cans dark sweet cherries in heavy syrup
1/4 cup sugar
1/4 cup cornstarch
Dash of salt
1 teaspoon butter
1 cup fresh blueberries
1/4 cup sugar
1 tablespoon cornstarch
Dash of salt
1 teaspoon butter
1 teaspoon lemon juice
2 (1-crust) pie pastries

Combine the cherries, 1/4 cup sugar, 1/4 cup cornstarch, dash of salt and 1 teaspoon butter in a 3-quart saucepan and mix well. Cook over medium heat until the mixture is thick and translucent. Remove from the heat to cool. Combine the blueberries, 1/4 cup sugar, 1 tablespoon cornstarch, dash of salt, 1 teaspoon butter and the lemon juice in a 2-quart saucepan and mix well. Cook over medium heat until the mixture is thick and translucent. Remove from the heat to cool.

Fit 1 of the pie pastries into a 9-inch pie plate. Cut and bend a 6-inch piece of cardboard or thick plastic to form a 90-degree-angle wedge. Place the wedge in the upper left quadrant of the pie (like the hands of a clock pointing to the 9 and 12). Fill this quarter of the pie with the blueberry mixture. Fill the remaining 3/4 of the pie with the cherry mixture. Remove the wedge.

Cut five 1/2-inch strips from the remaining pastry. Place 3 long strips evenly across the filling toward the bottom edge, beginning in the middle of the pie. Cut the remaining 2 strips into 4-inch pieces. Lay over the cherry filling in the upper right quadrant of the pie. Press the edges of the strips into the edges of the pie pastry, fluting or crimping the edge. Cut 5 or 6 stars from the remaining pastry and place on the blueberry quadrant. Bake at 425 degrees for 30 minutes. Reduce the oven temperature to 350 degrees. Bake for 25 to 30 minutes or until the pastry is golden brown and the filling bubbles. Remove to a wire rack and cool completely.

Rachel Gregory, Lebanon

Buttermilk Pie

1 tablespoon all-purpose flour
1 tablespoon cornmeal
3 eggs, lightly beaten
1 1/2 cups sugar
1/2 cup (1 stick) butter, melted
1/2 cup buttermilk
1 teaspoon vanilla extract
1 unbaked (9-inch) pie shell

Mix the flour and cornmeal in a bowl. Add the eggs, sugar, butter, buttermilk and vanilla and mix well. Pour into the pie shell. Bake at 350 degrees for 40 to 45 minutes or until set.

Sarah Jennings, Lebanon

Buttermilk Lemon Pie

1 (1-crust) pie pastry
1 cup sugar
3 tablespoons all-purpose flour
1/2 teaspoon salt
2 cups buttermilk
4 eggs, lightly beaten
1/4 cup (1/2 stick) butter, melted
1/3 cup lemon juice
1 tablespoon grated lemon zest
1 teaspoon vanilla extract
1 teaspoon ground nutmeg

Line a 9-inch pie plate with the pastry, trimming and fluting the edge. Mix the sugar, flour and salt in a large bowl. Beat the buttermilk, eggs, butter, lemon juice, lemon zest and vanilla in a large mixing bowl until smooth. Add to the sugar mixture and mix well. Pour into the prepared pie plate. Sprinkle with the nutmeg. Bake at 400 degrees for 10 minutes. Reduce the oven temperature to 325 degrees. Bake for 40 to 45 minutes or until a wooden pick inserted near the center comes out clean. Cool on a wire rack.

Rachel Gregory, Lebanon

Lime Coconut Buttermilk Pie

PASTRY

$1^{1}/_{3}$ cups all-purpose flour
$^{1}/_{4}$ teaspoon salt
$^{1}/_{3}$ cup lard
1 teaspoon butter flavoring
3 to 4 tablespoons cold water

PIE

$1^{1}/_{2}$ cups sugar
$^{3}/_{4}$ cup sweetened shredded coconut
$^{1}/_{2}$ cup buttermilk
$^{1}/_{2}$ cup unsweetened coconut milk
1 tablespoon all-purpose flour
2 eggs
2 egg yolks
$^{1}/_{2}$ teaspoon vanilla extract
Grated zest and juice of 1 lime
Pinch of salt

For the pastry, mix the flour and salt in a bowl. Cut in the lard until crumbly. Add the butter flavoring and water 1 tablespoon at a time, mixing with a fork until the mixture forms a ball. Roll the dough into a 12-inch circle on a lightly floured surface. Fit into a pie plate, trimming and fluting the edge.

For the pie, combine the sugar, coconut, buttermilk, coconut milk, flour, eggs, egg yolks, vanilla, lime zest, lime juice and salt in a large bowl and whisk until well mixed. Pour into the prepared pie plate. Bake at 350 degrees for 40 to 50 minutes or until the filling is set. Remove from the oven and cool at room temperature.

Angela Collom, Watertown

Dark Sweet Cherry Pie

2 cups sifted all-purpose flour
1 teaspoon salt
3/4 cup shortening
4 to 5 tablespoons cold water
2 (15-ounce) cans dark sweet cherries in heavy syrup
1/2 cup sugar
1/3 cup cornstarch
Dash of salt
1/2 cup sugar
1 tablespoon butter
3 or 4 drops of almond extract
2 tablespoons lemon juice
1 egg white, lightly beaten
Sugar for sprinkling

Mix the flour and 1 teaspoon salt in a mixing bowl. Cut in the shortening with a pastry blender until the mixture is the consistency of coarse cornmeal or tiny peas. Sprinkle with the cold water, mixing lightly with a fork to form a ball. Shape into a smooth flattened disk and wrap in plastic wrap. Chill for 30 minutes or longer. Drain the cherries, reserving 1 cup of the liquid. Mix 1/2 cup sugar, the cornstarch and a dash of salt in a medium saucepan. Stir in the reserved cherry liquid. Cook over medium heat until thickened and bubbly, stirring constantly. Continue to cook for 1 minute longer, stirring constantly. Remove from the heat. Stir in 1/2 cup sugar, the drained cherries, butter, almond extract and lemon juice.

Divide the pie pastry into 2 equal portions. Roll 1 portion into a 12-inch circle on a lightly floured surface. Fit into a 9-inch deep-dish pie plate. Pour the cherry mixture into the prepared pie plate. Roll the remaining pastry into a 12-inch circle on a lightly floured surface and cut into strips. Arrange lattice-fashion over the pie, trimming and fluting the edge. Brush the lattice top with the beaten egg white and sprinkle with sugar. Place the pie plate on a baking sheet and cover the edge with foil. (Do not use a crust protector shield because the pastry will stick to it.) Bake at 375 degrees for 25 minutes. Remove the foil. Bake for 25 to 30 minutes longer or until the pastry is golden brown. Cool on a wire rack before serving. You may also make a regular pie plus 1 miniature pie.

Kelly Gregory, Lebanon

Cherry Strawberry Pie

1 (14-ounce) can tart red cherries in juice
1 cup sugar
3 tablespoons cornstarch
1/4 teaspoon salt
3/4 cup sweetened strawberry purée
1 (16-ounce) package frozen cherries, thawed
2 tablespoons butter
1 (2-crust) pie pastry
Milk for brushing

Drain the canned cherries, reserving the juice. Sift the sugar, cornstarch and salt into a saucepan. Stir in the strawberry purée and reserved cherry juice. Cook over medium heat until smooth, stirring constantly. Add the canned and frozen cherries. Simmer until the mixture is thick and translucent, stirring gently several times. Remove from the heat. Add the butter and stir until melted. Let stand until cool.

Divide the pastry into 2 equal portions. Roll each portion into a 12-inch circle on a lightly floured surface. Fit 1 pastry into a 9-inch pie plate. Pour in the cool cherry mixture. Top with the remaining pastry, trimming and fluting the edge and cutting vents. Brush the top of the pastry with milk. Bake at 400 degrees for 45 minutes or until golden brown.

Tim White, Lebanon

Cherry Pie

2 (14-ounce) cans water-pack pitted tart red cherries
3/4 cup sugar
1/3 cup cornstarch
Dash of salt
3/4 cup sugar
1 tablespoon butter
3 or 4 drops of almond extract
10 drops of red food coloring
1 (2-crust) pie pastry
1 egg white, lightly beaten, or milk
Sugar for sprinkling

Drain the cherries, reserving 1 cup of the liquid. Mix 3/4 cup sugar, the cornstarch and salt in a medium saucepan. Stir in the reserved cherry liquid. Cook over medium heat until thickened and bubbly, stirring constantly. Continue to cook for 1 minute longer, stirring constantly. Remove from the heat. Stir in 3/4 cup sugar, the drained cherries, butter, almond extract and food coloring.

Divide the pie pastry into 2 equal portions. Roll 1 portion into a 12-inch circle on a lightly floured surface. Fit into a 9-inch deep-dish pie plate. Pour the cherry mixture into the prepared pie plate. Roll the remaining pastry into a 12-inch circle on a lightly floured surface and cut into strips. Arrange lattice-fashion over the pie, trimming and fluting the edge. Brush the lattice top with the egg white and sprinkle with sugar. Place the pie plate on a baking sheet and cover the edge with foil. (Do not use a crust protector shield because the pastry will stick to it.) Bake at 375 degrees for 25 minutes. Remove the foil. Bake for 25 to 30 minutes longer or until the pastry is golden brown. Cool on a wire rack before serving. You may also make a regular pie plus 1 miniature pie.

Rachel Gregory, Lebanon

Chess Pie

1$^1/_2$ cups sugar
$^1/_2$ cup (1 stick) butter, softened
1 teaspoon vinegar
3 eggs, lightly beaten
1 teaspoon vanilla extract
1 unbaked (9-inch) pie shell

Combine the sugar, butter and vinegar in a bowl and mix well with a wooden spoon. Add the eggs and vanilla and mix well. Pour into the pie shell. Bake at 350 degrees for 45 to 50 minutes or until set.

Robin Nation, Lebanon

Cornmeal Chess Pie

1 cup all-purpose flour
$^1/_2$ teaspoon salt
$^1/_3$ cup shortening
3 tablespoons cold water
1$^1/_4$ cups sugar
1 tablespoon cornmeal
1 tablespoon vinegar
Pinch of salt
3 eggs, lightly beaten
$^1/_2$ cup (1 stick) butter, softened
1 teaspoon vanilla extract

Mix the flour and $^1/_2$ teaspoon salt in a bowl. Cut in the shortening until crumbly. Add the water 1 tablespoon at a time, mixing with a fork until the mixture forms a ball. Chill, wrapped in plastic wrap, for 30 minutes or longer. Roll the pastry into a 12-inch circle on a lightly floured surface. Fit into a 9-inch pie plate, trimming and fluting the edge.

Mix the sugar, cornmeal, vinegar and a pinch of salt in a bowl. Add the eggs, butter and vanilla and mix well. Pour into the prepared pie plate. Bake at 350 degrees for 50 minutes or until set.

Mary Lou Ford, Lebanon

Old-Fashioned Chess Pie

3 eggs
1 tablespoon vinegar
1/4 cup milk
1 1/2 cups sugar
1 tablespoon cornmeal
2 teaspoons vanilla extract
1/2 cup (1 stick) butter, melted
1 unbaked (9-inch) pie shell

Combine the eggs, vinegar, milk, sugar, cornmeal and vanilla in a bowl and whisk until blended. Whisk in the butter and pour into the pie shell. Bake at 350 degrees for 45 minutes or until set.

Margaret Thompson Kilgore, Lebanon

Southern Chess Pie

1/2 cup (1 stick) margarine
1 1/2 cups sugar
3 eggs
1 1/2 teaspoons vinegar
1 teaspoon vanilla extract
1 tablespoon cornmeal
1 unbaked (9-inch) pie shell

Cream the margarine and sugar in a mixing bowl until light and fluffy. Add the eggs 1 at a time, beating well after each addition. Add the vinegar, vanilla and cornmeal and mix well. Pour into the unbaked pie shell. Bake at 325 degrees for 45 minutes or until set.

Russell Lane, Lebanon

Chocolate Chip Pie

1 cup sugar
1/2 cup all-purpose flour
1/2 cup (1 stick) margarine, melted and cooled
2 eggs, well beaten
1 teaspoon vanilla extract
1 cup (6 ounces) semisweet chocolate chips
1/2 cup chopped nuts
1 unbaked (9-inch) pie shell

Mix the sugar and flour in a bowl. Add the melted margarine, eggs and vanilla and mix well. Stir in the chocolate chips and nuts. Pour into the unbaked pie shell. Bake at 375 degrees for 10 minutes. Reduce the oven temperature to 350 degrees. Bake for 30 minutes or until firm.

Russell Lane, Lebanon

Chocolate Chip Cheese Pie

GRAHAM CRACKER CRUST

1 1/3 cups graham cracker crumbs (about 16 squares)
1/4 cup sugar
1/4 cup (1/2 stick) margarine, softened
1/4 teaspoon ground cinnamon

PIE

24 ounces cream cheese, softened
3/4 cup sugar
3 eggs
1 teaspoon vanilla extract
2 cups (12 ounces) miniature semisweet chocolate chips
2 tablespoons heavy cream or whipping cream

For the crust, combine the graham cracker crumbs, sugar, margarine and cinnamon in a bowl and mix until crumbly. Press evenly into a 9-inch pie plate, forming a small rim. Bake at 375 degrees for 8 minutes or until the edge is light brown. Cool on a wire rack.

For the pie, beat the cream cheese and sugar in a large mixing bowl for 5 minutes. Add the eggs and vanilla and beat well. Stir in 1 2/3 cups of the chocolate chips. Pour into the cooled piecrust. Bake at 375 degrees for 10 minutes. Reduce the oven temperature to 250 degrees and continue to bake for 30 minutes. Remove from the oven and cool completely on a wire rack. Cover and chill completely in the refrigerator.

Mix the remaining 1/3 cup chocolate chips and cream in a small microwave-safe bowl. Microwave on High for 20 to 30 seconds or until the chocolate chips are melted and the mixture is smooth when stirred. Cool slightly. Spread over the top of the pie. Chill for 15 minutes or until the topping is set. Store in the refrigerator.

Rachel Gregory, Lebanon

Best Chocolate Meringue Pie

PIE

1 1/2 cups sugar
3 tablespoons baking cocoa
6 tablespoons self-rising flour
4 egg yolks
1 1/2 cups milk
3 tablespoons butter
1 1/2 teaspoons vanilla extract
1 baked (9-inch) pie shell

MERINGUE

4 egg whites, at room temperature
1/4 teaspoon cream of tartar
1/4 cup sugar
1/4 teaspoon vanilla extract

For the pie, mix the sugar, baking cocoa and flour in a saucepan. Add the egg yolks and mix well. Add the milk gradually, stirring constantly. Cook over medium-high heat until thickened, stirring constantly. Remove from the heat. Add the butter and vanilla and mix well. Pour into the pie shell.

For the meringue, beat the egg whites and cream of tartar at high speed in a mixing bowl until soft peaks form. Add the sugar and vanilla gradually, beating until stiff peaks form. Spread over the pie, sealing to the edge. Bake at 325 degrees until the meringue is golden brown.

Shelia Farris, Lebanon

Chocolate Meringue Pie

PIE
1 cup sugar
3 tablespoons baking cocoa
2 tablespoons (heaping) all-purpose flour
3 egg yolks
1 1/4 cups milk
1 tablespoon butter
1 baked (9-inch) pie shell

MERINGUE
3 egg whites, at room temperature
2 teaspoons cold water
1/2 teaspoon cream of tartar
6 tablespoons sugar

For the pie, mix the sugar, baking cocoa and flour in a double boiler or cast-iron skillet. Stir in the egg yolks. Add the milk and butter and mix well. Cook until thickened, stirring constantly. Pour into the pie shell.

For the meringue, beat the egg whites, water and cream of tartar at high speed in a mixing bowl until soft peaks form. Add the sugar gradually, beating until stiff peaks form. Spread over the pie, sealing to the edge. Bake at 350 degrees until the meringue is brown.

Sarah Jennings, Lebanon

Favorite Chocolate Pie

PASTRY

1 1/2 cups all-purpose flour
1/4 teaspoon salt
1/2 cup shortening
3 tablespoons ice water

PIE

6 tablespoons baking cocoa
2 1/2 tablespoons all-purpose flour
2 tablespoons cornstarch
1 cup sugar
1/8 teaspoon salt
1/2 cup milk
3 egg yolks, lightly beaten
1 1/2 cups milk, scalded
2 tablespoons butter
1 teaspoon vanilla extract

MERINGUE

3 egg whites, at room temperature
1 teaspoon cream of tartar
6 tablespoons sugar

For the pastry, mix the flour and salt in a bowl. Cut in the shortening with a pastry blender until crumbly. Add the ice water 1 tablespoon at a time, mixing with your hands until the mixture forms a ball. Roll into a 12-inch circle on a floured pastry cloth. Fit into a pie plate, trimming and fluting the edge. Bake at 400 degrees until light brown. Cool on a wire rack.

For the pie, mix the baking cocoa, flour, cornstarch, sugar and salt in a saucepan. Stir in 1/2 cup milk and the egg yolks. Add 1 1/2 cups scalded milk. Cook until thickened, stirring constantly. Remove from the heat. Stir in the butter and vanilla. Let stand until cool. Pour into the cooled pastry.

For the meringue, beat the egg whites and cream of tartar at high speed in a mixing bowl until soft peaks form. Add the sugar gradually, beating until stiff peaks form. Spread over the pie, sealing to the edge. Bake at 350 degrees for 12 to 15 minutes or until the meringue is brown.

Delores Butler, Lebanon

Heavenly Chocolate Pie

PIE

1 cup sugar
1/4 cup all-purpose flour
3 tablespoons baking cocoa
3 egg yolks
1 1/2 cups milk
1/4 cup (1/2 stick) margarine
1 teaspoon vanilla extract
1 baked (9-inch) pie shell

MERINGUE

3 egg whites, at room temperature
1/4 teaspoon cream of tartar
6 tablespoons sugar

For the pie, mix the sugar, flour and baking cocoa in a double boiler. Beat the egg yolks into the milk in a bowl and add to the sugar mixture. Stir in the margarine and vanilla. Cook until thick and creamy, stirring frequently. Pour into the pie shell.

For the meringue, beat the egg whites and cream of tartar at high speed in a mixing bowl for 1 minute or until frothy. Add the sugar gradually, beating until stiff but not dry peaks form. Spread over the pie, sealing to the edge. Bake at 350 degrees until the meringue is brown.

Virginia Poston, Watertown

Old-Fashioned Chocolate Pie

PIE

3 egg yolks
1 1/2 cups milk
1 1/4 cups sugar
1/4 cup all-purpose flour
1/4 cup baking cocoa
1 teaspoon margarine
1 teaspoon vanilla extract
1 (7-ounce) jar marshmallow creme
1 baked (9-inch) pie shell

MERINGUE

3 egg whites, at room temperature
3 tablespoons sugar

For the pie, combine the egg yolks, milk, sugar, flour, baking cocoa, margarine, vanilla and marshmallow creme in a cast-iron skillet and mix well. Cook until thickened, stirring constantly. Pour into the pie shell.

For the meringue, beat the egg whites at high speed in a mixing bowl until soft peaks form. Add the sugar gradually, beating until stiff peaks form. Spread over the pie, sealing to the edge. Bake at 350 degrees until the meringue is golden brown.

Betty Worley, Lebanon

Best-Ever Fudge Pie

1 cup sugar
1/4 cup all-purpose flour
1/4 cup baking cocoa
2 eggs
1/2 cup (1 stick) margarine, melted
1 teaspoon vanilla extract
1 unbaked (9-inch) pie shell

Mix the sugar, flour and baking cocoa together. Beat the eggs lightly in a mixing bowl. Add the margarine and vanilla and mix well. Add the sugar mixture and mix well. Pour into the pie shell. Bake at 325 degrees for 25 to 30 minutes or until the filling is just firm.

Virginia Poston, Watertown

Fudge Pie

1 cup sugar
1/4 cup self-rising flour
3 tablespoons baking cocoa
1/2 cup (1 stick) butter, softened
2 eggs, beaten
1 teaspoon vanilla extract
1 unbaked (9-inch) pie shell

Mix the sugar, flour and baking cocoa in a bowl. Add the butter, eggs and vanilla and mix well. Pour into the pie shell. Bake at 325 degrees for 25 to 30 minutes or until the filling is firm.

Robin Nation, Lebanon

Fudge Pie with Homemade Pastry

PASTRY

4 cups all-purpose flour
1 tablespoon sugar
1 1/2 teaspoons salt
1 1/2 cups shortening
1 egg, beaten
1 teaspoon vinegar
1/2 cup (about) cold water

PIE

2 2/3 tablespoons margarine, melted
1 1/4 cups sugar
3 tablespoons baking cocoa
2 eggs
1/2 cup evaporated milk
1 teaspoon vanilla extract

For the pastry, mix the flour, sugar and salt in a bowl. Cut in the shortening until crumbly. Stir in the egg. Add the vinegar and water and mix well to form a ball. Knead well on a floured surface. Roll into a 10-inch circle. Fit into a pie plate, trimming and fluting the edge.

For the pie, combine the margarine, sugar and baking cocoa in a bowl and stir to mix well. Stir in the eggs. Do not beat. Add the evaporated milk and vanilla and stir to mix well. Pour into the prepared pie plate. Bake at 400 degrees for 10 minutes. Reduce the oven temperature to 350 degrees. Bake for 20 to 25 minutes or until the pastry is brown.

Caryn Crowston, Mt. Juliet

Walnut Fudge Pie

2/3 cup evaporated milk
2 tablespoons butter
1 cup (6 ounces) semisweet chocolate chips
2 eggs, beaten
1 cup sugar
2 tablespoons all-purpose flour, sifted
3/4 teaspoon salt
2 teaspoons vanilla extract
1 cup chopped black walnuts
1 unbaked (9-inch) pie shell

Combine the evaporated milk, butter and chocolate chips in a microwave-safe container. Microwave on High until melted, stirring after 1 or 2 minutes. Let stand until cool. Add the eggs and stir to mix well. Mix the sugar and flour in a large bowl. Stir in the chocolate mixture, salt, vanilla and walnuts. Pour into the pie shell. Bake at 375 degrees for 35 minutes. Serve warm.

Rachel Gregory, Lebanon

Coconut Pie

3 eggs
1 1/2 cups sugar
1 tablespoon vinegar or lemon juice
1/2 cup (1 stick) margarine, melted
1 teaspoon vanilla extract
1/3 cup shredded coconut
Pinch of salt
1 unbaked (9-inch) pie shell

Beat the eggs in a mixing bowl. Stir in the sugar, vinegar, margarine, vanilla, coconut and salt. Pour into the pie shell. Bake at 350 to 375 degrees for 45 minutes or until set.

Amy Upchurch, Watertown

French Coconut Pie

PIE PASTRY

1 cup all-purpose flour
1/2 teaspoon salt
Pinch of baking powder
1/3 cup shortening
2 tablespoons cold water

PIE

3 eggs
1 1/2 cups sugar
1/4 cup (1/2 stick) butter, melted
6 tablespoons buttermilk
1 teaspoon vanilla extract
1 cup shredded coconut

For the pastry, mix the flour, salt and baking powder in a bowl. Cut in the shortening until crumbly. Add the water 1 tablespoon at a time, mixing with a fork until the dough forms a ball. Roll into a 12-inch circle on a lightly floured surface. Fit into a pie plate, trimming and fluting the edge.

For the pie, combine the eggs, sugar, butter, buttermilk and vanilla in a bowl and mix well. Stir in the coconut. Pour into the prepared pie plate. Bake at 325 degrees for 30 minutes.

Ruth Snodgrass, Mt. Juliet

Coconut Cream Pie

PIE

1/2 cup cornstarch
1 1/3 cups sugar
1 teaspoon salt
4 3/4 cups milk
5 egg yolks, beaten
1 teaspoon vanilla extract
1 cup flaked coconut
1 baked (9-inch) pie shell

MERINGUE

5 egg whites, at room temperature
3/4 cup sugar
Flaked coconut (optional)

For the pie, mix the cornstarch, sugar and salt in a double boiler. Stir in the milk gradually. Cook over boiling water until thick enough to mound slightly when dropped from a spoon, stirring constantly. Cover and cook for 10 minutes longer, stirring occasionally. Stir a small amount of the mixture into the egg yolks. Stir the egg yolks into the hot mixture. Cook for 3 minutes, stirring constantly. Remove from the heat. Stir in the vanilla and coconut. Pour into the pie shell.

For the meringue, beat the egg whites at high speed in a mixing bowl until foamy. Add the sugar a small amount at a time, beating well after each addition. Continue to beat until stiff peaks form. Spread over the pie, sealing to the edge. Sprinkle with additional coconut. Bake at 350 degrees for 15 minutes or until the top is golden brown.

Barb Oxley, Lebanon

Wonderful Coconut Cream Pie

PIE

1 (1-crust) pie pastry
1 cup sugar
1/4 cup cornstarch
1/4 teaspoon salt
3 cups milk
4 egg yolks
3 tablespoons butter
1 1/2 teaspoons vanilla extract
1 (3-ounce) can flaked coconut

MERINGUE

4 egg whites, at room temperature
1/2 teaspoon vanilla extract
1/4 teaspoon cream of tartar
6 tablespoons sugar
Flaked coconut for sprinkling

For the pie, roll the pastry into a 12-inch circle on a lightly floured surface. Fit into a 9-inch pie plate, trimming the pastry to 1/2-inch beyond the edge and folding over. Flute the edge of the pastry and prick with a fork. Bake at 450 degrees for 10 to 12 minutes or until golden brown. Cool on a wire rack.

Mix the sugar, cornstarch and salt in a saucepan. Stir in the milk gradually. Cook until thickened and bubbly, stirring constantly. Pour a small amount of the hot mixture into the beaten egg yolks. Stir the egg yolks into the hot mixture. Reduce the heat and cook for 2 minutes, stirring constantly. Remove from the heat. Stir in the butter and vanilla. Stir in the coconut. Pour into the baked pie shell.

For the meringue, beat the egg whites, vanilla and cream of tartar at medium speed in a medium mixing bowl for 1 minute or until medium peaks form. Add the sugar gradually, beating at high speed for 4 minutes or until the mixture forms stiff glossy peaks and the sugar is dissolved. Spread immediately over the hot filling, carefully sealing to the edge. Sprinkle with coconut. Bake at 350 degrees for 12 to 15 minutes or until the meringue is golden brown. Let stand until cool. Cover and store in the refrigerator.

Rachel Gregory, Lebanon

Mile-High Coconut Meringue Pie

PIE

1 cup sugar
3 tablespoons cornstarch
1/4 teaspoon salt
2 cups half-and-half
4 egg yolks
3 tablespoons butter
1/2 teaspoon vanilla extract
1/2 cup shredded coconut
1 baked (9-inch) pie shell

MERINGUE

4 egg whites, at room temperature
1/2 teaspoon cream of tartar
1/3 cup sugar
1/2 teaspoon vanilla extract

For the pie, sift the sugar, cornstarch and salt into a medium saucepan. Add the half-and-half. Cook over medium heat until thickened, stirring constantly. Remove from the heat. Stir a small amount of the hot mixture into the egg yolks. Stir the egg yolks into the hot mixture. Bring to a rolling boil over medium heat, stirring constantly. Continue to cook for 2 minutes. Remove from the heat and stir in the butter and vanilla. Stir in the coconut and pour into the pie shell.

For the meringue, beat the egg whites and cream of tartar at high speed in a mixing bowl for 1 minute. Add the sugar 1 tablespoon at a time, beating constantly. Add the vanilla and beat until stiff peaks form. Spread over the pie, sealing to the edge. Bake at 325 degrees until the meringue is light brown.

Tim White, Lebanon

Coconut Meringue Pie

PIE
1 cup sugar
2 tablespoons (heaping) all-purpose flour
3 egg yolks, beaten
1 1/4 cups milk
2 tablespoons butter
1 cup flaked coconut
1 baked (9-inch) pie shell

MERINGUE
3 egg whites, at room temperature
2 teaspoons cold water
1/2 teaspoon cream of tartar
6 tablespoons sugar
Flaked coconut for sprinkling

For the pie, mix the sugar, flour and egg yolks in a double boiler or cast-iron skillet. Add the milk and butter. Cook until thickened, stirring constantly. Remove from the heat to cool. Stir in the coconut and pour into the pie shell.

For the meringue, beat the egg whites, water and cream of tartar at high speed in a mixing bowl until thick. Add the sugar gradually, beating constantly until stiff peaks form. Spread over the pie, sealing to the edge. Sprinkle with coconut. Bake at 350 degrees until the meringue is brown.

Sarah Jennings, Lebanon

Japanese Fruit Pie

PASTRY

1 cup sifted all-purpose flour
1/2 teaspoon salt
6 tablespoons shortening
3 tablespoons cold water

PIE

6 tablespoons butter, softened
1 cup sugar
2 eggs, well beaten
1/2 cup chopped pecans
1/2 cup raisins
1/2 cup shredded coconut
1 teaspoon vanilla extract
1 teaspoon vinegar

For the pastry, mix the flour and salt in a mixing bowl. Cut in the shortening with a pastry blender until the mixture is the consistency of coarse cornmeal or tiny peas. Sprinkle with the water and mix with a fork until a dough is formed. Shape into a smooth flattened disk and wrap in plastic wrap. Chill for 30 minutes or longer. Roll the pastry into a 12-inch circle on a lightly floured surface. Fit into a 9-inch pie plate, trimming and fluting the edge.

For the pie, cream the butter and sugar in a mixing bowl until light and fluffy. Stir in the eggs, pecans, raisins, coconut, vanilla and vinegar. Pour into the prepared pie plate. Bake at 350 degrees for 40 minutes.

Rachel Gregory, Lebanon

Lemon Meringue Pie

PIE

1 cup sugar
3 tablespoons cornstarch
1/4 teaspoon salt
2 cups half-and-half
4 egg yolks, beaten
3 tablespoons butter
1/2 teaspoon vanilla extract
1/3 cup lemon juice
1 teaspoon lemon zest
1 baked (9-inch) pie shell

MERINGUE

4 egg whites, at room temperature
1/2 teaspoon cream of tartar
1/3 cup sugar
1/2 teaspoon vanilla extract

For the pie, sift the sugar, cornstarch and salt into a medium saucepan. Stir in the half-and-half. Cook over medium heat until thickened, stirring constantly. Remove from the heat. Stir a small amount of the hot mixture into the egg yolks. Stir the egg yolks into the hot mixture. Bring to a rolling boil over medium heat, stirring constantly. Continue to cook for 2 minutes, stirring constantly. Remove from the heat and stir in the butter and vanilla. Stir in the lemon juice and lemon zest and pour into the pie shell.

For the meringue, beat the egg whites and cream of tartar at high speed in a mixing bowl for 1 minute. Add the sugar 1 tablespoon at a time, beating constantly. Add the vanilla and beat until stiff peaks form. Spread over the pie, sealing to the edge. Bake at 325 degrees until the meringue is light brown.

Tim White, Lebanon

Icebox Lemon Meringue Pie

1 1/2 cups sifted all-purpose flour
1/2 teaspoon salt
1/2 cup shortening
1/4 cup ice water
1 1/2 cups sugar
1/3 cup cornstarch
1 3/4 cups water
5 egg yolks, lightly beaten
1 1/2 tablespoons butter
1 tablespoon lemon juice
5 egg whites, at room temperature
3/4 cup sugar

Mix the flour and salt in a mixing bowl. Cut in the shortening using a pastry blender until crumbly. The mixture should be fairly coarse. Add 1/4 cup ice water 1 tablespoon at a time, mixing with a fork until the mixture forms a ball. Shape the dough into a firm ball. Roll into a 10 1/2-inch circle on a lightly floured surface. Fit into a 9-inch pie plate, trimming and fluting the edge. Bake at 425 degrees for 15 minutes. Mix 1 1/2 cups sugar and the cornstarch in a double boiler. Stir in 1 3/4 cups water gradually. Cook over boiling water for 7 to 9 minutes or until thickened and clear, stirring constantly. Stir 1/2 cup of the hot mixture into the egg yolks. Stir the egg yolks into the hot mixture. Cook for 3 minutes, stirring constantly. Remove from the heat. Add the butter and lemon juice gradually, mixing thoroughly after each addition. Pour into the baked pie shell.

Beat the egg whites at high speed in a mixing bowl until foamy. Add 3/4 cup sugar a small amount at a time, beating well after each addition. Continue beating until stiff peaks form. Spread over the pie, sealing to the edge. Bake at 350 degrees for 15 minutes. Cool at room temperature for 1 hour. Chill for 3 to 4 hours before serving.

Barb Oxley, Lebanon

Zesty Lemon Meringue Pie

PIE

1 3/4 cups sugar
1/4 cup cornstarch
3 tablespoons flour
1/4 teaspoon salt
2 cups water
4 egg yolks, lightly beaten
1/3 cup lemon juice
1 tablespoon grated lemon zest
1 tablespoon butter
1 baked (9-inch) pie shell

MERINGUE

4 egg whites, at room temperature
1/4 teaspoon cream of tartar
1/2 cup sugar

For the pie, mix the sugar, cornstarch, flour and salt in a saucepan. Stir in the water. Bring to a boil over medium heat, stirring until smooth. Boil for 1 minute or until shiny or translucent. Remove from the heat and add a small amount of the hot mixture to the egg yolks. Stir the egg yolks into the hot mixture. Cook over low heat for 5 minutes, stirring constantly. Remove from the heat. Stir in the lemon juice, lemon zest and butter. Pour into the pie shell.

For the meringue, beat the egg whites and cream of tartar at medium speed in a mixing bowl until frothy. Add the sugar gradually, beating well after each addition. Beat at high speed until stiff peaks form. Spread over the pie, sealing to the edge. Bake at 400 degrees for 7 to 9 minutes or until the meringue is golden brown.

Laura Doucette, Mt. Juliet

Fresh Peach Pie

PASTRY
2 cups all-purpose flour
1 teaspoon salt
1/2 cup corn oil
1/4 cup milk

PIE
7 cups sliced peeled peaches
1/4 cup tapioca
3/4 cup sugar
1 tablespoon lemon juice
1 teaspoon almond extract
1 tablespoon butter
Milk for brushing

For the pastry, mix the flour and salt together in a bowl and make a well in the center. Pour the corn oil and milk into the well and stir to form a dough. Divide the dough into 2 equal portions. Roll each portion into a 12-inch circle. Fit 1 portion into a 9-inch pie plate.

For the pie, combine the peaches, tapioca, sugar, lemon juice and almond extract in a bowl and mix well. Let stand for 15 minutes. Spoon into the prepared pie plate and dot with the butter. Moisten the edge of the pie pastry with milk. Top with the remaining pastry, trimming and fluting the edge. Cut vents in the top of the pastry to allow steam to escape. Cover the pastry edge with foil. Bake at 435 degrees for 10 minutes. Reduce the oven temperature to 350 degrees. Bake for 40 minutes longer. Remove the foil and bake for 10 minutes longer.

Rita Spradling, Lebanon

Miscellaneous Peach Fruit Pie

3/4 cup all-purpose flour
1 teaspoon baking powder
1/2 teaspoon salt
1 egg
1/2 cup milk
1 (4-ounce) package vanilla cook-and-serve pudding mix
3 tablespoons margarine, softened
1 (16- to 20-ounce) can peaches
8 ounces cream cheese, softened
1/2 cup plus 1 tablespoon sugar
1/2 teaspoon ground cinnamon

Combine the flour, baking powder, salt, egg, milk, pudding mix and margarine in a mixing bowl and beat at medium speed for 2 minutes. Pour into a buttered 9-inch pie plate. Drain the peaches, reserving 3 tablespoons of the juice. Arrange the peaches over the batter.

Beat the cream cheese, 1/2 cup of the sugar and the reserved peach juice in a mixing bowl for 2 minutes. Spoon over the peaches to about 1 inch from the edge. Sprinkle with a mixture of the remaining 1 tablespoon sugar and the cinnamon. Bake at 350 degrees for 30 to 35 minutes or until set.

Mary Lou Ford, Lebanon

Old-Fashioned Peach Pie

1 (2-crust) pie pastry
5 cups sliced fresh peaches
1 teaspoon lemon juice
3/4 cup sugar
3 tablespoons all-purpose flour
1/4 teaspoon ground cinnamon or nutmeg
1/8 teaspoon salt
2 tablespoons butter

Divide the pastry into 2 equal portions. Roll 1 portion into a 12-inch circle on a lightly floured surface. Fit into a 9-inch pie plate. Combine the peaches and lemon juice in a bowl and toss to coat. Mix the sugar, flour, cinnamon and salt together. Add to the peaches, stirring to coat. Pour into the prepared pie plate and dot with the butter. Roll the remaining pastry into a 12-inch circle on a lightly floured surface and cut into strips. Arrange lattice-fashion over the pie, either folding the strips under the pastry edge or pressing into the pastry edge and fluting the edge. Bake at 425 degrees for 40 to 50 minutes or until the pastry is brown.

Rachel Gregory, Lebanon

Peach Cheesecake Pie

PASTRY

1 cup sifted all-purpose flour
1/8 teaspoon salt
1/2 cup (1 stick) butter, softened
3 ounces cream cheese, softened

GLAZE

1/2 cup sugar
1 teaspoon cornstarch
1/2 cup water
1 peach, mashed

PIE

1 (14-ounce) can sweetened condensed milk
8 ounces cream cheese, softened
1/3 cup lemon juice
1 teaspoon vanilla extract
4 peaches, sliced

For the pastry, mix the flour and salt together. Cream the butter and cream cheese in a mixing bowl until light and fluffy. Add the flour mixture 1/2 at a time, mixing thoroughly after each addition. Shape into a flattened disk and wrap in plastic wrap. Chill until the pastry can be easily handled. Unwrap the pastry and roll into a 12-inch circle on a lightly floured surface. Fit into a 9-inch pie plate, trimming and fluting the edge. Bake at 450 degrees for 12 minutes or until light brown. Cool completely on a wire rack.

For the glaze, combine the sugar, cornstarch, water and peach in a saucepan. Cook over medium heat until thickened and translucent, stirring constantly. Remove from the heat to cool completely.

For the pie, combine the condensed milk, cream cheese, lemon juice and vanilla in a mixing bowl and beat until smooth. Pour into the pastry-lined pie plate. Arrange the peach slices over the cream cheese mixture. Spread the glaze over the top. Chill or freeze until ready to serve.

Rachel Gregory, Lebanon

Peanut Butter Pie

2 eggs
1 cup sugar
1 teaspoon vanilla extract
1/2 cup (1 stick) butter, softened
1/4 cup all-purpose flour
1 cup peanut butter
1 unbaked (9-inch) pie shell

Combine the eggs, sugar, vanilla, butter, flour and peanut butter in a mixing bowl and beat until smooth. Pour into the pie shell. Bake at 350 degrees for 25 minutes.

Mary Lou Ford, Lebanon

Dark Pecan Pie

3 eggs
1 cup sugar
1 cup dark corn syrup
1/4 cup (1/2 stick) butter, melted
1 teaspoon vanilla extract
1 cup (or more) pecans
1 unbaked (9-inch) pie shell

Combine the eggs, sugar and corn syrup in a mixing bowl and beat well. Add the butter and vanilla and mix well. Stir in the pecans. Pour into the pie shell. Bake at 350 degrees for 45 minutes or until set.

Sarah Jennings, Lebanon

Pecan Pie

3 eggs
1 cup corn syrup
1 cup sugar
2 tablespoons butter
1 teaspoon vanilla extract
1¼ cups pecans
1 unbaked (9-inch) pie shell

Combine the eggs, corn syrup, sugar, butter and vanilla in a mixing bowl and mix well. Stir in the pecans. Pour into the pie shell. Bake at 350 degrees for 50 minutes or until set.

Robin Nation, Lebanon

Southern Pecan Pie

1 cup sugar
2 tablespoons flour
1/2 teaspoon salt
2 tablespoons milk
1 teaspoon vanilla extract
2 eggs
1/2 cup corn syrup
1/2 cup shortening, melted
1 unbaked (9-inch) pie shell
1/2 cup broken pecans

Mix the sugar, flour and salt in a bowl. Add the milk and vanilla and mix well. Add the eggs 1 at a time, beating well after each addition. Add the corn syrup and shortening and mix well. Pour into the pie shell and sprinkle with the pecans. Bake at 300 degrees for 50 minutes or until set.

Mary Preston, Lebanon

Million-Dollar Pineapple Pie

GRAHAM CRACKER CRUST

4 cups graham cracker crumbs (48 to 54 crackers)
3/4 cup sugar
3/4 teaspoon ground cinnamon
3/4 cup (1 1/2 sticks) margarine, softened

PIE

1 (20-ounce) can crushed pineapple, drained
1 (14-ounce) can sweetened condensed milk
1/4 cup lemon juice
15 ounces whipped topping
3/4 cup chopped nuts

For the crust, combine the graham cracker crumbs, sugar, cinnamon and margarine in a bowl and mix until crumbly. Divide into 3 equal portions. Press each portion evenly into a 9-inch pie plate, forming a small rim. Bake at 375 degrees for 8 minutes or until the edges are light brown. Cool on wire racks.

For the pie, combine the pineapple, condensed milk and lemon juice in a large bowl and mix well. Fold in the whipped topping and nuts. Spoon into the baked piecrusts. Chill for 2 hours or longer before serving or freeze.

Kelly Gregory, Lebanon

Pineapple Pie

PIE

3 eggs
1/4 cup (1/2 stick) butter
1 small can crushed pineapple
1 cup sugar
3 tablespoons all-purpose flour
1 baked (9-inch) pie shell

MERINGUE

1 egg white
2 tablespoons sugar

For the pie, combine the eggs, butter, pineapple, sugar and flour in a saucepan and mix well. Cook until thickened, stirring constantly. Pour into the pie shell.

For the meringue, beat the egg white at high speed in a mixing bowl until soft peaks form. Add the sugar gradually, beating constantly until stiff peaks form. Cover the pie with the meringue, sealing to the edge. Bake at 350 degrees until brown.

Mary Lou Ford, Lebanon

Pumpkin Pie

2 eggs, lightly beaten
1 (16-ounce) can solid-pack pumpkin
3/4 cup sugar
1/2 teaspoon salt
1 teaspoon ground cinnamon
1/2 teaspoon ginger
1/4 teaspoon ground cloves
1 1/2 cups evaporated milk
1 unbaked (9-inch) pie shell

Mix the eggs, pumpkin, sugar, salt, cinnamon, ginger, cloves and evaporated milk in the order listed in a bowl. Pour into the pie shell. Bake at 425 degrees for 15 minutes. Reduce the oven temperature to 350 degrees. Bake for 45 minutes longer or until a knife inserted in the center comes out clean.

Laura S. Doucette, Mt. Juliet

Pumpkin Silk Pie

CRUST
2 cups rolled oats
1 1/2 cups all-purpose flour, sifted
1 cup (2 sticks) butter, melted
1/2 cup firmly packed brown sugar

PIE
16 ounces cream cheese, softened
1 (16-ounce) can pumpkin
1 1/2 cups confectioners' sugar, sifted
2 teaspoons vanilla extract
2 teaspoons ground cinnamon
1/2 teaspoon nutmeg
1/2 teaspoon ginger
2 cups whipped topping
1/4 cup coarsely chopped pecans

For the crust, mix the oats, flour, butter and brown sugar in a large bowl. Press evenly in the bottom and up the side of a lightly greased 9-inch pie plate. Bake at 375 degrees for 12 to 15 minutes or until golden brown. Cool on a wire rack.

For the pie, combine the cream cheese, pumpkin, confectioners' sugar, vanilla, cinnamon, nutmeg and ginger in a mixing bowl and beat at medium speed for 5 minutes or until smooth. Fold in the whipped topping. Spread in the baked piecrust. Sprinkle the top with the pecans. Chill for 3 to 12 hours before serving.

Rachel Gregory, Lebanon

Ritz Cracker Pie

3 egg whites, at room temperature
1 cup sugar
1/2 teaspoon baking powder
16 Ritz crackers, crumbled
2/3 cup pecan pieces
1/2 teaspoon vanilla extract
Whipped cream or whipped topping

Beat the egg whites at high speed in a mixing bowl until soft peaks form. Add the sugar and baking powder gradually, beating until stiff peaks form. Fold in the crackers, pecans and vanilla. Pour into a well-greased pie plate. Bake at 350 degrees for 25 minutes. Remove from the oven and let stand at room temperature to cool. Chill in the refrigerator for several hours. Cover with whipped cream and serve.

Sarah Jennings, Lebanon

Strawberry Rhubarb Pie

1 1/4 cups sugar
3 tablespoons quick-cooking tapioca
3 cups strawberries, sliced
2 cups (1/4- to 1/2-inch) sliced rhubarb
1/2 teaspoon finely shredded orange zest
1/2 teaspoon ground cinnamon
1/4 teaspoon nutmeg
1 (2-crust) pie pastry

Combine the sugar and tapioca in a large mixing bowl and mix well. Add the strawberries, rhubarb, orange zest, cinnamon and nutmeg and toss until the strawberries and rhubarb are coated. Let stand for 15 minutes or until a syrup forms, stirring occasionally.

Divide the pastry into 2 equal portions. Roll each portion into a 12-inch circle on a lightly floured surface. Fit 1 portion into a 9-inch pie plate. Fill with the fruit mixture. Cut the remaining pastry portion into strips. Arrange lattice-fashion over the pie, trimming and fluting the edge. Bake at 375 degrees for 45 to 50 minutes or until the top is golden brown.

Rachel Gregory, Lebanon

Blackberry Cobbler

2 tablespoons butter
1 cup all-purpose flour
1 cup sugar
1 cup milk
2 cups blackberries
Sugar for sprinkling

Melt the butter in an 8×8-inch baking pan in a 375-degree oven. Maintain the oven temperature. Combine the flour, 1 cup sugar and the milk in a bowl and mix well. Pour over the melted butter. Add the blackberries. Bake for 45 minutes. Sprinkle sugar over the top.

Kathy Settle, Lebanon

Double-Crust Blackberry Cobbler

PASTRY
2 cups all-purpose flour
1 teaspoon salt
2/3 cup plus 2 tablespoons shortening
4 to 5 tablespoons cold water

COBBLER
1 quart blackberries
1 cup sugar
1 teaspoon all-purpose flour
1/4 cup (1/2 stick) butter, melted
Sugar for sprinkling
Pat of butter

For the pastry, mix the flour and salt in a bowl. Cut in the shortening with a pastry blender until the mixture resembles coarse cornmeal. Add the water 1 tablespoon at a time, mixing with a fork until the dry ingredients are moistened. Shape into a ball and wrap in plastic wrap. Chill in the refrigerator.

For the cobbler, mix the blackberries, 1 cup sugar, the flour and 1/4 cup butter in a bowl until evenly mixed. Divide the pastry into 2 equal portions. Roll each portion into a rectangle. Fit 1 portion into the bottom of a number nine 1 1/2-inch-deep aluminum baking pan. Spoon in the blackberry mixture. Top with the remaining pastry, cutting vents. Sprinkle with sugar and add a pat of butter. Bake at 350 degrees for 45 minutes.

Charline Smith, Lebanon

Blueberry Cobbler

2 tablespoons butter
1 cup sugar
1 cup self-rising flour
1 cup milk
1 (21-ounce) can blueberry pie filling
Sugar for sprinkling

Melt the butter in an 8×8-inch baking pan in a 375-degree oven. Maintain the oven temperature. Combine 1 cup sugar, the flour and milk in a bowl and mix well. Pour over the melted butter. Spoon the blueberry pie filling over the batter. Bake for 45 minutes. Sprinkle with sugar.

Kathy Settle, Lebanon

Kay's Favorite Cobbler

1/2 cup (1 stick) butter
1 3/4 cups sugar
2 cups water
1 1/2 cups sifted self-rising flour
1/2 cup shortening
1/3 cup milk
2 cups blueberries

Melt the butter in a 9×13-inch baking dish in a 350-degree oven. Maintain the oven temperature. Heat the sugar and water in a saucepan until the sugar melts.

Cut the flour into the shortening in a bowl until fine crumbs form. Add the milk and stir with a fork until the dough leaves the side of the bowl. Knead the dough on a lightly floured board or pastry cloth until smooth. Roll into a large rectangle about 1/4 inch thick. Sprinkle evenly with the blueberries. Roll up as for a jelly roll, dampening the edges with a little warm water to seal. Cut the roll into 16 slices about 1/2 inch thick. Place in the melted butter. Pour the sugar syrup carefully around the rolls. (The crust will absorb the liquid.) Bake for 55 to 60 minutes or until golden brown.

You may also make this pie using fresh, frozen or canned fruit, such as blackberries, cherries or peaches. If the fruit is packed in liquid, drain and use for part of the sugar syrup, making sure you always use 2 cups of liquid.

Kay McCrary, Lebanon

Peach Cobbler

1 recipe biscuit dough
1 quart peaches
1/4 cup (1/2 stick) butter
Sugar to taste
Sugar for sprinkling

Roll the biscuit dough into a thin circle. Cut with a biscuit cutter and place 1/2 of the dough circles in a baking pan. Heat the peaches and butter in a saucepan until the butter melts. Add sugar to taste. Pour into the prepared pan. Top with the remaining dough circles and sprinkle with sugar. Bake at 350 degrees for 45 to 50 minutes or until golden brown.

Pat Byrant, Lebanon

Easy Peach Cobbler

$5^1/_3$ tablespoons butter
1 cup self-rising flour
$^1/_2$ cup sugar
Dash of ground cinnamon
1 teaspoon vanilla extract
$^1/_2$ cup milk
1 quart sweetened peaches

Melt the butter in an 8×8-inch baking dish in a 350-degree oven. Maintain the oven temperature.

Stir the flour, sugar, cinnamon, vanilla and milk into the melted butter. Pour the peaches over the top. Bake for 1 hour.

Tammy Rice, Lebanon

Rhubarb Cobbler

3 cups diced rhubarb
1 cup sugar
1 tablespoon butter
1/2 cup shortening
1 cup sugar
1 egg
1 cup self-rising flour
1/2 cup milk

Place the rhubarb in a 9×12-inch baking dish and sprinkle with 1 cup sugar. Dot with the butter. Cream the shortening and 1 cup sugar in a mixing bowl until light and fluffy. Beat in the egg. Add the flour and milk and mix well. Drop by tablespoonfuls over the rhubarb. Bake at 350 degrees for 1 hour. Serve warm with whipped cream or ice cream.

Rachel Gregory, Lebanon

Fruit Cobbler

2 cups fruit
Sugar to taste
1/2 cup (1 stick) butter, melted
1/2 cup all-purpose flour
1/2 cup milk
1/2 cup sugar
Sugar for sprinkling
Butter

Heat the fruit with sugar to taste in a saucepan. Combine 1/2 cup butter, the flour, milk and 1/2 cup sugar in a bowl and mix well. Pour into an 8-inch baking dish. Pour the fruit over the batter. Sprinkle with sugar and dot with butter. Bake at 375 degrees for 30 minutes.

Mary Lou Ford, Lebanon

Fried Peach Pies

1 package dried peaches
3/4 cup water
1/2 cup sugar
3 tablespoons shortening
1 cup plus 2 tablespoons self-rising flour
1/2 cup buttermilk
1 tablespoon white vinegar
Vegetable oil for frying

Place the peaches and water in a 1-quart saucepan. Cover and let stand for 2 hours. Cook over low heat for 45 minutes. Remove from the heat and stir in the sugar. Let stand for 15 minutes. Pour into a strainer and drain for 5 minutes.

Cut the shortening into the flour in a 1 1/2-quart mixing bowl until crumbly. Blend the buttermilk and vinegar in a 1-cup measure. Add to the flour mixture, stirring with a fork until moistened and the dough is smooth and holds together. Shape into a ball. Sift a thin layer of flour onto a pastry cloth. Roll the dough 1/8 inch thick, sprinkling the surface and rolling pin with flour as needed. Cut the dough into 6-inch circles. Knead the scraps of dough together and repeat until all of the dough is used.

Spread 1/2 of each circle with the drained peaches to within 1/2 inch of the edge. Fold over and crimp with the tines of a fork to enclose the filling. Fry in hot oil in a skillet until golden brown.

Charline Smith, Lebanon

Fresh Peach Fried Pies

2 cups sifted all-purpose flour
1 teaspoon salt
3/4 cup shortening
4 to 5 tablespoons cold water
5 medium or 4 large peaches, peeled and cut into slices
2/3 cup sugar
1 tablespoon apple cider vinegar
1 cup (or more) shortening for frying

Mix the flour and salt in a mixing bowl. Cut in 3/4 cup shortening with a pastry blender until the mixture resembles coarse cornmeal or tiny peas. Add the water 1 tablespoon at a time, mixing with a fork until the mixture forms a ball. Shape into a smooth flattened disk and wrap in plastic wrap. Chill for 30 minutes or longer.

Bring the peaches, sugar and vinegar to a boil in saucepan and reduce the heat to low. Simmer, with the lid slightly ajar, for 2 hours, stirring occasionally. Drain in a colander or strainer for 30 minutes or until the peaches are the consistency of peach preserves.

Roll the pastry 1/8 inch thick on a lightly floured surface. Cut into 12 circles about 4 inches in diameter. Spread about 1 tablespoon of the peach mixture on 1/2 of each circle to within 1/2 inch from the edge. Fold each circle in half. Moisten the rims of each circle with cold water and crimp the edges with the tines of a fork to enclose the filling. Prick with the tines of a fork. Fry in 1 cup shortening in a skillet for 4 to 5 minutes on each side or until light brown, adding additional shortening as needed.

Rachel Gregory, Lebanon

Peach Fried Pies

1 package dried peaches or your favorite fruit
3/4 cup water
Sugar to taste
1/4 cup shortening
1 1/2 cups self-rising flour
1/3 cup milk
Vegetable oil for frying

Cook the dried peaches in the water in a saucepan until soft. Stir in sugar to taste. Process in a blender until smooth.

Cut the shortening into the flour in a bowl until crumbly. Add the milk and stir to form a stiff dough. Divide the dough into small equal pieces. Roll each piece into a thin circle.

Spread 2 to 3 tablespoons of the peaches on 1/2 of each circle. Fold each circle over and crimp with a fork to enclose the filling. Prick each with a fork to allow steam to escape. Fry in oil in an electric skillet at 350 degrees until golden brown. Remove to paper towels to drain. Serve hot or cold. Store completely cooled pies in a container with waxed paper between layers.

Kay McCrary, Lebanon

Easy Pie Pastry

1 cup all-purpose flour
1/2 teaspoon salt
1/3 cup shortening
2 to 3 tablespoons ice water

Mix the flour and salt in a bowl. Cut in the shortening until crumbly. Add the water 1 tablespoon at a time, mixing with a fork until the mixture is moistened. Shape into a ball and wrap in plastic wrap. Chill for 1 hour. Roll into a 12-inch circle on a lightly floured surface. Fit into a 9-inch pie plate, trimming and fluting the edge. This recipe freezes well.

Leasa Gammon, Lebanon

Quick Breads

Nutty Banana Bread

2 cups all-purpose flour
1 teaspoon baking soda
1/2 teaspoon salt
2/3 cup vegetable oil
1 1/4 cups sugar
3 large bananas, mashed
2 eggs, lightly beaten
1/2 cup chopped nuts
1/2 cup buttermilk
1 teaspoon vanilla extract

Mix the flour, baking soda and salt in a bowl. Add the oil, sugar, bananas, eggs, nuts, buttermilk and vanilla in the order listed, mixing well after each addition. Spoon the batter into a greased 5×9-inch loaf pan and bake at 350 degrees for 1 hour. Cool in the pan for 10 minutes and invert onto a wire rack to cool completely.

Sarah Jennings, Lebanon

Banana Walnut Bread

1 cup sugar
$^1/_2$ cup (1 stick) margarine
2 eggs
3 bananas, mashed
$1^1/_2$ cups all-purpose flour
1 cup walnuts, chopped

Beat the sugar, margarine, eggs and bananas in a mixing bowl until blended. Add the flour and stir just until moistened. Fold in the walnuts. Spoon the batter into a greased 5×9-inch loaf pan and bake at 350 degrees for 1 hour. Cool in the pan for 10 minutes and invert onto a wire rack to cool completely.

Brenda Whitehead, Watertown

Hawaiian Banana Bread

3 cups all-purpose flour
2 cups sugar
2 teaspoons ground cinnamon
1 teaspoon baking soda
1 teaspoon salt
3 eggs, well beaten
2 cups mashed ripe bananas
1 cup vegetable oil
1 (8-ounce) can crushed pineapple
1 cup chopped nuts
1 cup raisins
1 teaspoon vanilla extract

Mix the flour, sugar, cinnamon, baking soda and salt in a bowl. Combine the eggs, bananas, oil, undrained pineapple, nuts, raisins and vanilla in a bowl and mix well. Add the flour mixture to the banana mixture and stir until moistened.

Spoon the batter evenly into two 5×9-inch loaf pans sprayed with nonstick cooking spray. Bake at 350 degrees for 1 hour or until a wooden pick inserted in the centers comes out clean. Cool in the pans for 10 minutes and invert onto a wire rack to cool completely.

Jan Rich, Mt. Juliet

Buttermilk Banana Nut Bread

1 teaspoon baking soda
1 cup buttermilk
3 cups all-purpose flour
1 teaspoon baking powder
3/4 cup shortening
1 3/4 cups sugar
3 eggs, beaten
1/2 teaspoon vanilla extract
3 bananas, mashed
1 cup chopped nuts

Dissolve the baking soda in the buttermilk in a bowl. Sift the flour and baking powder together. Beat the shortening and sugar in a mixing bowl until creamy. Add the eggs and vanilla to the creamed mixture and beat until blended. Add the flour mixture and buttermilk mixture alternately, mixing until moistened after each addition. Fold in the bananas and nuts.

Spoon the batter evenly into two 5×9-inch loaf pans and bake at 350 degrees for 45 to 60 minutes or until the loaves test done. Cool in the pans for 10 minutes and invert onto a wire rack to cool completely.

Nancy Robinson, Lebanon

Banana Nut Bread

3 very ripe bananas
1 1/2 cups self-rising flour
1 cup sugar
1/4 cup (1/2 stick) butter, melted
1 egg, lightly beaten
1/2 cup chopped nuts

Mash the bananas in a bowl with a fork. Stir in the flour, sugar, butter, egg and nuts. Spoon the batter into a greased 4×8-inch loaf pan and bake at 350 degrees for 45 to 55 minutes or until the loaf tests done. Cool in the pan for 10 minutes and invert onto a wire rack to cool completely.

Kathy Settle, Lebanon

Apple Pumpkin Bread

$1^2/_3$ cups all-purpose flour
2 teaspoons ground cinnamon
1 teaspoon nutmeg
1 teaspoon baking soda
$^3/_4$ teaspoon salt
$^1/_4$ teaspoon baking powder
$^1/_4$ teaspoon ground cloves
$1^1/_2$ cups sugar
1 cup canned pumpkin
$^1/_2$ cup water
$^1/_3$ cup vegetable oil
2 eggs
1 cup chopped peeled Granny Smith apple
1 cup chopped walnuts

Combine the flour, cinnamon, nutmeg, baking soda, salt, baking powder and cloves in a bowl and mix well. Combine the sugar, pumpkin, water, oil and eggs in a mixing bowl and beat until blended. Add the flour mixture to the pumpkin mixture and beat at low speed just until moistened, scraping the bowl occasionally. Fold in the apple and walnuts.

Spoon the batter into a greased 5×9-inch loaf pan and bake at 325 degrees for $1^1/_2$ to $1^3/_4$ hours or until a wooden pick inserted in the center comes out clean. Cool in the pan for 10 minutes and invert onto a wire rack to cool completely.

Jan Rich, Mt. Juliet

Pumpkin Bread

5 cups all-purpose flour
4 teaspoons baking soda
1 teaspoon ground cinnamon
1 teaspoon ground allspice
1/2 teaspoon salt
2 eggs
4 cups sugar
2 1/2 cups canned pumpkin
1 cup vegetable oil
2 cups chopped nuts

Mix the flour, baking soda, cinnamon, allspice and salt in a bowl. Beat the eggs in a mixing bowl until blended. Add the sugar, pumpkin and oil to the eggs and beat until smooth. Beat in the flour mixture just until moistened and fold in the nuts.

Spoon the batter into a greased 5×9-inch loaf pan and bake at 350 degrees for 50 to 60 minutes or until the loaf tests done. Cool in the pan for 10 minutes and invert onto a wire rack to cool completely.

Kathy Settle, Lebanon

Pumpkin Ribbon Bread

CREAM CHEESE FILLING

6 ounces cream cheese, softened
1/3 cup sugar
1 tablespoon all-purpose flour
1 egg
2 teaspoons grated orange zest

PUMPKIN BREAD

1 2/3 cups all-purpose flour
1 teaspoon baking soda
1 cup canned pumpkin
1/3 cup vegetable oil
2 eggs
1 1/2 cups sugar
1/2 teaspoon salt
1/2 teaspoon ground cloves
1/2 teaspoon ground cinnamon
1 cup chopped pecans

For the filling, beat the cream cheese, sugar and flour in a mixing bowl until creamy. Add the egg and beat until blended. Stir in the orange zest.

For the bread, mix the flour and baking soda together. Combine the pumpkin, oil and eggs in a bowl and mix until blended. Stir in the sugar, salt, cloves and cinnamon. Add the flour mixture and stir until blended. Fold in the pecans.

Spread 1/2 of the batter in a greased and floured 5×9-inch loaf pan and spread with the filling. Top with the remaining batter and bake at 325 degrees for 1 1/2 hours or until a wooden pick inserted in the center comes out clean and the top is golden brown. Cool in the pan for 10 minutes and invert onto a wire rack to cool completely.

Jan Rich, Mt. Juliet

Spiced Pumpkin Bread

3 1/2 cups all-purpose flour
2 teaspoons baking soda
2 teaspoons salt
1 teaspoon baking powder
1 teaspoon nutmeg
1 teaspoon ground allspice
1 teaspoon ground cinnamon
1/2 teaspoon ground cloves
3 cups sugar
1 cup vegetable oil
1 (16-ounce) can pumpkin
4 eggs, beaten
2/3 cup water

Sift the flour, baking soda, salt, baking powder, nutmeg, allspice, cinnamon and cloves into a bowl and mix well. Beat the sugar and oil in a mixing bowl until creamy. Add the pumpkin and eggs to the creamed mixture and beat until blended. Add the flour mixture and water alternately, mixing just until moistened after each addition.

Spoon the batter evenly into 2 greased and floured 5×9-inch loaf pans and bake at 350 degrees for 1 1/2 hours or until the loaves test done. Cool in the pans for 10 minutes and invert onto a wire rack to cool completely.

Mallissa Bolton, Lebanon

Easy Strawberry Bread

1 1/2 cups self-rising flour
1 cup sugar
1/4 cup butter, melted
1 egg, lightly beaten
1/2 cup chopped fresh strawberries

Combine the flour, sugar, butter and egg in a bowl and mix well. Fold in the strawberries. Spoon the batter into a greased 5×9-inch loaf pan and bake at 350 degrees for 1 hour. Cool in the pan for 10 minutes and invert onto a wire rack to cool completely.

Kathy Settle, Lebanon

Strawberry Bread

2 cups sifted all-purpose flour
1 teaspoon baking soda
1 cup sugar
1/2 cup (1 stick) butter, softened
2 eggs, beaten
1 cup chopped strawberries
1 cup finely chopped nuts

Sift the flour and baking soda together. Beat the sugar and butter in a mixing bowl until creamy and fold in the eggs. Stir in the strawberries and flour mixture and fold in the nuts.

Spoon the batter into a greased and lightly floured 5×9-inch loaf pan and let stand for 20 minutes. Bake at 350 degrees for 35 to 40 minutes or until the loaf tests done.

Mary Lou Ford, Lebanon

Best-Ever Strawberry Bread

3 cups all-purpose flour
2 teaspoons baking soda
1 teaspoon salt
2 cups sugar
4 eggs
1 1/4 cups vegetable oil
1 tablespoon ground cinnamon
2 cups chopped strawberries

Mix the flour, baking soda and salt together. Combine the sugar and eggs in a mixing bowl and beat until blended. Beat in the oil and cinnamon. Add the flour mixture and beat just until moistened. Fold in the strawberries.

Spoon the batter evenly into 2 greased loaf pans and bake at 350 degrees for 1 1/4 hours. Cool in the pans for 10 minutes and invert onto a wire rack to cool completely.

Mary Lena Price, Lebanon

Cinnamon Strawberry Bread

2 (10-ounce) packages frozen sliced strawberries, thawed
3 cups all-purpose flour
2 cups sugar
1 tablespoon ground cinnamon
1 teaspoon baking soda
1 teaspoon salt
1 1/4 cups vegetable oil
3 eggs, beaten

Line the bottom of two 5×9-inch loaf pans with foil and lightly grease the foil and sides of the pans. Drain the strawberries, reserving the juice. Combine the flour, sugar, cinnamon, baking soda and salt in a bowl and mix well. Make a well in the center of the flour mixture. Add the oil and eggs to the well and stir just until moistened.

Gently stir the strawberries into the batter. Add the reserved juice until the desired consistency is reached and mix well. Spoon the batter evenly into the prepared pans and bake at 350 degrees for 1 hour or until the loaves test done. Cool in the pans for 15 minutes. Run a sharp knife around the edges of the loaves and invert onto a wire rack. Let stand until cool.

Jan Rich, Mt. Juliet

Strawberry Bread with Strawberry Glaze

BREAD

2 (16-ounce) packages frozen strawberries, thawed
6 tablespoons sugar
2 cups all-purpose flour
1 teaspoon baking powder
1 teaspoon baking soda
1 teaspoon ground cinnamon
1/4 teaspoon salt
1 1/2 cups sugar
1/2 cup shortening
2 eggs
1 teaspoon vanilla extract
1 cup finely chopped pecans

STRAWBERRY GLAZE

1 cup confectioners' sugar
2 tablespoons butter, melted
1 teaspoon vanilla extract

For the bread, drain the strawberries, reserving the juice for the glaze. Process the strawberries and 6 tablespoons sugar in a blender until puréed; the mixture should yield approximately 2 1/4 cups. Mix the flour, baking powder, baking soda, cinnamon and salt in a bowl.

Beat 1 1/2 cups sugar and the shortening in a mixing bowl until creamy. Add the eggs and vanilla and beat until blended. Add the creamed mixture to the flour mixture and stir just until moistened. Fold in the strawberry purée and the pecans. Spoon the batter into 2 greased and floured 5×9-inch loaf pans and bake at 325 degrees for 55 to 60 minutes or until the loaves test done. Cool in the pans for 10 minutes and invert onto a wire rack to cool completely.

For the glaze, combine the confectioners' sugar, butter and vanilla in a mixing bowl and beat until smooth. Add the reserved juice 1 tablespoon at a time until the desired consistency is reached, mixing well after each addition. Drizzle over the cooled loaves.

Susan Wright, Mt. Juliet

Zucchini Bread

3 cups all-purpose flour
1 tablespoon ground cinnamon
1 teaspoon baking soda
1 teaspoon salt
1/4 teaspoon baking powder
2 cups sugar
1 cup vegetable oil
3 eggs
2 teaspoons vanilla extract
3 cups shredded zucchini

Mix the flour, cinnamon, baking soda, salt and baking powder together. Combine the sugar, oil, eggs and vanilla in a mixing bowl and beat until blended. Add the flour mixture and stir just until moistened. Fold in the zucchini.

Spoon the batter evenly into 2 greased 5×9-inch loaf pans and bake at 325 degrees for 1 hour. Cool in the pans for 10 minutes and invert onto a wire rack to cool completely.

Tonya Kirby, Mt. Juliet

Applesauce Zucchini Bread

2 cups sugar
1 cup vegetable oil
3 eggs
1 cup applesauce
3 cups self-rising flour
1 tablespoon ground cinnamon
1 teaspoon vanilla extract
1 cup pecans, chopped
2 cups grated unpeeled zucchini

Beat the sugar, oil and eggs in a mixing bowl until smooth. Add the applesauce and beat until blended. Stir in the flour, cinnamon and vanilla. Stir in the pecans and fold in the zucchini.

Spoon the batter into 2 greased 5×9-inch loaf pans and bake at 350 degrees for 45 minutes. Cool in the pans for 10 minutes and invert onto a wire rack to cool completely.

Mary Lena Price, Lebanon

Cinnamon Zucchini Bread

3 cups all-purpose flour
2 tablespoons ground cinnamon
2 cups sugar
1 cup vegetable oil
3 eggs
1 teaspoon vanilla extract
2 cups grated zucchini

Mix the flour and cinnamon together. Combine the sugar, oil, eggs and vanilla in a mixing bowl and beat until blended. Add the flour mixture and beat just until moistened. Fold in the zucchini.

Spoon the batter into 2 greased 5×9-inch loaf pans and bake at 325 degrees for 1 hour. Cool in the pans for 10 minutes and invert onto a wire rack to cool completely.

Brenda Whitehead, Watertown

Nutty Zucchini Bread

3 cups all-purpose flour
1 tablespoon baking powder
1 tablespoon ground cinnamon
1 teaspoon baking soda
1 teaspoon salt
1 3/4 cups sugar
1 cup vegetable oil
3 eggs
2 cups grated zucchini
1 cup chopped nuts
1 teaspoon vanilla extract

Mix the flour, baking powder, cinnamon, baking soda and salt together. Combine the sugar, oil and eggs in a mixing bowl and beat until blended. Add the flour mixture and beat just until moistened. Fold in the zucchini, nuts and vanilla.

Spoon the batter evenly into 2 greased 4×8-inch loaf pans and bake at 350 degrees for 1 hour or until the loaves test done.

Scott Hobbs, Lebanon

Pineapple Zucchini Bread

3 cups self-rising flour
1 1/2 teaspoons ground cinnamon
1 teaspoon baking soda
3/4 cup chopped nuts
2 cups sugar
1 cup vegetable oil
3 eggs
2 teaspoons vanilla extract
2 cups shredded partially peeled zucchini
1 (8-ounce) can crushed pineapple, drained

Mix the flour, cinnamon and baking soda in a bowl and stir in the nuts. Combine the sugar, oil, eggs and vanilla in a mixing bowl and beat until blended. Add the flour mixture and mix just until moistened. Fold in the zucchini and pineapple.

Spoon the batter into 2 or 3 greased loaf pans and bake at 350 degrees for 1 hour or until the loaves test done. Cool in the pans for 10 minutes and invert onto a wire rack to cool completely.

Margaret Thompson Kilgore, Lebanon

Cinnamon Rolls

1/4 cup plus 1/2 teaspoon shortening
3 cups self-rising flour
1 cup milk
1/2 cup (1 stick) butter, softened
1/2 cup granulated sugar
1/2 cup firmly packed brown sugar
1 tablespoon ground cinnamon
1/2 cup confectioners' sugar
3 tablespoons milk

Cut the shortening into the flour in a bowl until crumbly. Add 1 cup milk and mix with a fork until the dough leaves the side of the bowl. Knead the dough 4 to 6 times on a lightly floured surface and roll into a 14×20-inch rectangle.

Spread the butter over the rectangle, leaving a narrow border on each side. Mix the granulated sugar, brown sugar and cinnamon in a bowl and sprinkle over the butter. Roll as for a jelly roll, beginning with the long side. Pinch the edge and ends to seal.

Cut the roll into 1-inch slices and arrange the slices cut side down in a greased 9×13-inch baking pan. Bake at 375 degrees for 20 to 25 minutes or until light brown. Cool in the pan on a wire rack. Drizzle with a mixture of the confectioners' sugar and 3 tablespoons milk.

Robin Nation, Lebanon

Pumpkin Spice Roll

PUMPKIN CAKE

Confectioners' sugar to taste
3/4 cup all-purpose flour
1 1/2 teaspoons pumpkin pie spice
1 teaspoon baking powder
1/4 teaspoon salt
1 cup granulated sugar
3 eggs
3/4 cup canned pumpkin
1 cup chopped walnuts

CREAM CHEESE FILLING AND ASSEMBLY

2 cups confectioners' sugar
8 ounces cream cheese, softened
1/2 cup chopped walnuts (optional)
Confectioners' sugar (optional)

For the cake, grease a 10×15-inch jelly roll pan. Line the pan with waxed paper and grease and flour the waxed paper. Liberally sprinkle a large clean kitchen towel with confectioners' sugar. Mix 3/4 cup flour, the pumpkin pie spice, baking powder and salt in a bowl.

Beat the granulated sugar and eggs in a mixing bowl at high speed until thickened. Add the pumpkin and beat until blended. Add the flour mixture and mix just until moistened. Spread the batter in the prepared pan and sprinkle with the walnuts. Bake at 375 degrees for 15 minutes or until the top springs back when lightly touched. Immediately invert onto the prepared towel and remove the pan. Carefully remove the waxed paper. Roll up in the towel, starting at the narrow end. Remove to a wire rack to cool.

For the filling, beat the confectioners' sugar and cream cheese in a mixing bowl until light and fluffy. Stir in the walnuts. Carefully unroll the cake and remove the towel. Spread the filling over the cake and roll to enclose the filling. Wrap the roll tightly in plastic wrap and chill for 1 hour or until serving time. Sprinkle the roll with confectioners' sugar and cut as desired. The roll may be stored, covered, in the refrigerator for several days.

Harriet Cummings, Lebanon

Pumpkin Roll

PUMPKIN CAKE

3/4 cup granulated sugar
2 eggs
3/4 cup canned pumpkin
1/2 cup self-rising flour
1 teaspoon vanilla extract
3/4 teaspoon baking soda
1/2 cup chopped nuts
Confectioners' sugar for sprinkling

CREAM CHEESE FILLING AND ASSEMBLY

8 ounces cream cheese, softened
1 cup confectioners' sugar
2 tablespoons margarine
1 teaspoon vanilla extract

For the cake, beat the granulated sugar and eggs in a mixing bowl until combined. Add the pumpkin, flour, vanilla and baking soda and beat until blended. Spread the batter in a greased 10×15-inch jelly roll pan and sprinkle with the nuts. Bake at 375 degrees for 12 to 15 minutes or until the cake tests done. Invert the warm cake onto a sheet of waxed paper sprinkled with confectioners' sugar. Roll as for a jelly roll. Chill in the refrigerator until cool.

For the filling, beat the cream cheese, confectioners' sugar, margarine and vanilla in a mixing bowl until of a spreading consistency. Unroll the cake and discard the waxed paper. Spread the filling over the cake and reroll to enclose the filing. Chill in the refrigerator until serving time. Slice as desired.

Scott Hobbs, Lebanon

Basic Tender Muffins

2 1/2 cups all-purpose flour
3/4 cup sugar
2 teaspoons baking powder
1/2 teaspoon salt
1/2 teaspoon baking soda
1 cup buttermilk
2 eggs
1/2 cup (1 stick) butter, melted

Mix the flour, sugar, baking powder, salt and baking soda in a bowl. Whisk the buttermilk, eggs and butter in a bowl until blended. Add the buttermilk mixture to the flour mixture and stir just until moistened.

Spoon the batter evenly into 12 greased muffin cups and bake at 400 degrees for 20 to 25 minutes or until golden brown. Cool in the pan on a wire rack for 3 minutes and remove to a wire rack.

For Blueberry Orange Muffins, add 1 tablespoon grated orange zest, 1/2 teaspoon ground cinnamon and 1/8 teaspoon ground nutmeg to the flour mixture. Fold 1 1/2 cups blueberries into the batter and bake as directed above.

Ann Sharp, Watertown

Blueberry Muffins

3 cups all-purpose flour
1 tablespoon baking soda
1 teaspoon salt
2/3 cup shortening
1 cup sugar
3 eggs
1 cup milk
2 cups blueberries

Sift the flour, baking soda and salt together. Beat the shortening and sugar in a mixing bowl until creamy. Add the eggs and beat until blended. Add the flour mixture and milk alternately to the creamed mixture and mix just until moistened after each addition. Fold in the blueberries.

Fill greased muffin cups 2/3 full. Bake at 375 degrees for 15 to 20 minutes or until the muffins test done. Cool in the pan for 2 minutes and remove to a wire rack.

Mary Lou Ford, Lebanon

Ruth's Blueberry Muffins

2 cups all-purpose flour
1/2 cup sugar
1 tablespoon baking powder
1/2 teaspoon salt
1 cup milk
1/4 cup (1/2 stick) butter or margarine, melted
1 egg, lightly beaten
2/3 cup blueberries
2 tablespoons all-purpose flour

Combine 2 cups flour, the sugar, baking powder and salt in a bowl and mix well. Add the milk, butter and egg and stir just until moistened. Toss the blueberries and 2 tablespoons flour in a bowl. Fold the coated blueberries into the batter.

Fill lightly greased muffin cups 3/4 full and bake at 375 degrees for 20 to 25 minutes or until the muffins test done. Cool in the pan for 2 minutes and remove to a wire rack.

Ruth Manning, Lebanon

Fresh Blueberry Muffins

1 1/2 cups all-purpose flour
1 tablespoon baking powder
1/4 teaspoon salt
2/3 cup sugar
1/3 cup butter or margarine, softened
2 eggs
1 1/2 teaspoons vanilla extract
2/3 cup milk
1 1/2 cups fresh blueberries
Sugar for sprinkling

Mix the flour, baking powder and salt together. Beat 2/3 cup sugar and the butter in a mixing bowl for 1 minute. Add the eggs and vanilla and beat until smooth. Add 1/2 of the flour mixture to the creamed mixture and beat just until blended. Add the milk and remaining flour mixture and beat just until moistened. Fold in the blueberries.

Fill greased or paper-lined muffin cups 2/3 full and bake at 360 degrees for 20 to 25 minutes or until the muffins test done and are golden brown. Sprinkle the warm muffins with sugar. Cool for 2 minutes and remove to a wire rack.

Margaret Thompson Kilgore, Lebanon

Blueberry Cream Muffins

CREAM CHEESE FILLING

8 ounces cream cheese, softened
1/3 cup sugar
1 egg
1/8 teaspoon salt

MUFFINS

4 cups all-purpose flour
1 cup sugar
2 tablespoons baking powder
1 teaspoon salt
2 cups milk
1/2 cup (1 stick) butter or margarine, melted
2 eggs
2 cups fresh or frozen blueberries

For the filling, beat the cream cheese, sugar, egg and salt in a mixing bowl until light and fluffy.

For the muffins, mix the flour, sugar, baking powder and salt in a bowl. Beat the milk, butter and eggs in a mixing bowl until blended. Add the flour mixture and stir just until moistened. Fold in the blueberries.

Spoon 2 rounded tablespoons of the batter into greased muffin cups. Top each with 1 tablespoon of the filling and spread with the remaining batter. Bake at 375 degrees for 18 to 20 minutes or until a wooden pick inserted in the centers comes out clean. Cool in the pan for 10 minutes and remove to a wire rack.

Kathleen Taylor, Watertown

Bran Muffins

$1\frac{1}{4}$ cups all-purpose flour
$\frac{3}{4}$ cup sugar
1 teaspoon baking powder
1 teaspoon baking soda
$\frac{1}{2}$ teaspoon salt
$1\frac{1}{4}$ cups buttermilk
1 cup bran
$\frac{1}{4}$ cup vegetable oil
1 egg, beaten

Combine the flour, sugar, baking powder, baking soda and salt in a bowl and mix well. Mix the buttermilk and bran in a bowl and let stand for 5 minutes or until softened. Stir the oil and egg into the buttermilk mixture. Add the flour mixture and stir just until moistened.

Grease only the bottoms of 12 muffin cups and fill $\frac{3}{4}$ full with batter. Bake at 400 degrees for 18 to 20 minutes or until the muffins test done. Cool in the pan for 2 minutes and remove to a wire rack.

Caryn Crowston, Mt. Juliet

Refrigerator Bran Muffins

16 ounces bran
5 cups all-purpose flour
3 cups sugar
1 cup raisins
5 teaspoons baking soda
2 teaspoons salt
4 eggs, beaten
1 quart buttermilk
1 cup vegetable oil

Combine the bran, flour, sugar, raisins, baking soda and salt in a bowl and mix well. Make a well in the bran mixture. Whisk the eggs, buttermilk and oil in a bowl until blended and add to the well, stirring just until moistened.

Fill greased muffin cups 2/3 full and bake at 350 degrees for 20 minutes. Cool in the pan for 2 minutes and remove to a wire rack. Store the batter, covered, in the refrigerator for up to 5 weeks, baking as needed, if desired.

Alicia Hovies, Lebanon

Six-Week Bran Muffins

1 (15-ounce) package Raisin Bran cereal
4 cups all-purpose flour
3 cups sugar
1 tablespoon baking soda
2 teaspoons salt
1 quart buttermilk
1 cup vegetable oil
4 eggs, beaten
2 tablespoons ground cinnamon

Combine the cereal, flour, sugar, baking soda and salt in a bowl and mix well. Whisk the buttermilk, oil, eggs and cinnamon in a bowl until blended. Add the buttermilk mixture to the cereal mixture and stir just until moistened.

Fill greased muffin cups 2/3 full and bake at 400 degrees for 15 to 20 minutes or until the muffins test done. Cool in the pan for 2 minutes and remove to a wire rack. You may store the batter, covered, in the refrigerator for up to 6 weeks.

Petra Mitchell, Watertown

Cornmeal Muffins

2 cups self-rising cornmeal
1 3/4 cups buttermilk
1/4 cup shortening, melted, or vegetable oil

Combine the cornmeal, buttermilk and shortening in a bowl and mix just until moistened. Fill muffin cups 2/3 full and bake at 450 degrees for 10 to 12 minutes or until the muffins test done. Cool in the pan for 2 minutes and remove to a wire rack.

Patricia Wilson-Knihtila, Mt. Juliet

Sweet Cornmeal Muffins

2 cups self-rising cornmeal
2 tablespoons sugar
1 3/4 cups buttermilk
2 tablespoons vegetable oil
1 egg

Grease muffin cups and heat in a 475-degree oven until hot. Mix the cornmeal and sugar in a bowl. Whisk the buttermilk, oil and egg in a bowl until blended and stir into the cornmeal mixture just until moistened.

Fill the preheated muffin cups 2/3 full and bake for 20 minutes or until golden brown. Cool in the pan for 2 minutes and remove to a wire rack.

Betty Weatherby, Lebanon

Yummy Cornmeal Muffins

2 cups self-rising cornmeal
1 teaspoon sugar
1 egg
1 1/4 cups milk
1/4 cup bacon drippings

Grease muffin cups and heat in a 450-degree oven until hot. Mix the cornmeal and sugar in a bowl. Whisk the egg, milk and bacon drippings in a bowl until blended. Add the cornmeal mixture to the egg mixture and stir just until moistened.

Fill the preheated muffin cups 2/3 full and bake for 15 to 20 minutes or until the muffins test done. Cool in the pan for 2 minutes and remove to a wire rack.

Mary Lou Ford, Lebanon

Corn Muffins

1 cup cornmeal
1 cup all-purpose flour
1/4 cup sugar
1 tablespoon baking powder
1/2 teaspoon salt
1 cup milk
1 egg
1/4 cup shortening, melted

Sift the cornmeal, flour, sugar, baking powder and salt into a bowl and mix well. Whisk the milk, egg and shortening in a bowl until blended. Add the cornmeal mixture to the milk mixture and stir just until moistened.

Fill greased muffin cups 2/3 full and bake at 425 degrees for 20 to 25 minutes or until the muffins test done. Cool in the pan for 2 minutes and remove to a wire rack.

Tammy Rice, Lebanon

Homemade Biscuits

2 cups all-purpose flour
1 tablespoon baking powder
1 teaspoon salt
1/4 cup shortening
3/4 cup buttermilk
Melted butter for brushing (optional)

Mix the flour, baking powder and salt in a bowl and cut in the shortening until crumbly. Add the buttermilk and stir until the dough pulls away from side of the bowl. Knead gently on a lightly floured surface. Roll the dough 1/2 inch thick and cut into rounds with a biscuit cutter.

Arrange the rounds on a lightly greased baking sheet and bake for 8 to 10 minutes or until golden brown. Brush the tops with melted butter and serve immediately.

Margaret Thompson Kilgore, Lebanon

Buttermilk Biscuits

2 cups all-purpose flour
1 tablespoon baking powder
1/8 teaspoon baking soda
6 tablespoons shortening
1 1/4 cups buttermilk

Mix the flour, baking powder and baking soda in a bowl and cut in the shortening until crumbly. Add the buttermilk and stir until blended. Roll or pat the dough 1/2 inch thick on a lightly floured surface. Cut into rounds with a biscuit cutter.

Arrange the rounds on a lightly greased baking sheet and bake at 450 degrees for 10 to 15 minutes or until brown. Serve immediately.

Delores Butler, Lebanon

Self-Rising Buttermilk Biscuits

1/4 cup shortening
2 cups self-rising flour
1 1/4 cups buttermilk

Cut the shortening into the flour in a bowl until crumbly. Add the buttermilk and stir until blended. Knead the dough on a lightly floured surface 2 or 3 times or until smooth. Roll 1/2 inch thick and cut into rounds with a biscuit cutter.

Arrange the rounds with sides not touching on a lightly greased baking sheet and bake at 475 degrees for 10 minutes or until light brown. Serve immediately.

Betty Weatherby, Lebanon

Biscuits

1/3 cup shortening
2 cups self-rising flour
3/4 cup milk

Cut the shortening into the flour in a bowl until crumbly. Add the milk and stir until a soft dough forms. Knead the dough lightly on a lightly floured surface and roll 1/2 inch thick. Cut into rounds with a biscuit cutter.

Arrange the rounds on a lightly greased baking sheet and bake at 450 degrees for 10 to 12 minutes or until golden brown. Serve immediately.

Robin Nation, Lebanon

Stick Corn Bread

Vegetable oil for coating
Cornmeal for coating
2 cups cornmeal
2 cups self-rising flour
2 cups buttermilk
1/4 cup canola oil

Coat a cast-iron corn stick pan with oil and sprinkle with cornmeal for coating. Combine 2 cups cornmeal, the flour, buttermilk and canola oil in a bowl and mix well. Spoon the batter into the prepared pan and bake at 400 degrees for 45 minutes or until brown. Serve immediately.

Betty R. Kemp, Lebanon

Buttermilk Corn Bread

2 cups cornmeal
2 teaspoons sugar
1 3/4 cups buttermilk
1/4 cup vegetable oil

Mix the cornmeal and sugar in a bowl. Add the buttermilk and oil to the cornmeal mixture and stir until blended. Fill greased muffin cups 2/3 full and bake at 450 degrees for 15 to 20 minutes or until golden brown.

Leasa Gammon, Lebanon

Coffee Cake

STARTER MIX
1/2 cup all-purpose flour
1/2 cup sugar
1/2 cup milk

COFFEE CAKE
2 cups self-rising flour
1 (4-ounce) package any flavor instant pudding mix
3/4 cup vegetable oil
3/4 cup milk
3 eggs, beaten
1 teaspoon vanilla extract
1 cup jam, jelly or preserves
1 cup sugar
2 tablespoons ground cinnamon

For the starter mix, mix the flour and sugar in a bowl and stir in the milk. Let stand at room temperature for 8 to 12 hours.

For the coffee cake, mix the flour and pudding mix in a bowl. Add 1 cup of the starter mix, the oil, milk, eggs, vanilla and jam and stir just until moistened. Fill muffin cups sprayed with nonstick cooking spray 2/3 full and sprinkle evenly with a mixture of the sugar and cinnamon. Bake at 325 degrees for 35 minutes. You may bake in 2 loaf pans or a 9×13-inch cake pan for 1 hour.

Mary Lou Ford, Lebanon

Fat-Free Apple Coffee Cake

1 cup all-purpose flour
1 1/2 teaspoons baking powder
1/2 teaspoon salt
3/4 cup sugar
1/3 cup skim milk
2 egg whites
1/3 cup light or dark corn syrup
2 apples, peeled and cut into 1/2-inch wedges
2 tablespoons cinnamon-sugar

Mix the flour, baking powder and salt in a bowl. Whisk the sugar and skim milk in a bowl until combined. Add the egg whites and corn syrup and whisk until blended. Gradually add the flour mixture and stir until smooth.

Spread the batter in a 9-inch round baking pan sprayed with nonstick cooking spray. Overlap the apples over the top to cover and sprinkle with the cinnamon-sugar. Bake at 350 degrees for 50 minutes or until a wooden pick inserted in the center comes out clean. Cool in the pan on a wire rack. Cut into wedges to serve.

June Thomas, Lebanon

Blueberry Coffee Cake

2 cups fresh or frozen blueberries
3 cups all-purpose flour
1 teaspoon baking powder
1/2 teaspoon baking soda
1/2 teaspoon salt
2 cups granulated sugar
4 ounces 1/3-less-fat cream cheese, softened
1/3 cup butter or margarine, softened
3 eggs
1 egg white
2 teaspoons vanilla extract
8 ounces low-fat lemon yogurt
1/2 cup sifted confectioners' sugar
4 teaspoons lemon juice

Toss the blueberries and 2 tablespoons of the flour in a bowl until coated. Mix the remaining flour, baking powder, baking soda and salt in a bowl. Beat the granulated sugar, cream cheese and butter in a mixing bowl at medium speed until creamy. Add the eggs and egg white 1 at a time, beating well after each addition. Beat in the vanilla. Add the flour mixture and yogurt alternately to the creamed mixture, beating well after each addition and beginning and ending with the flour mixture. Fold in the blueberry mixture.

Spread the batter in a 10-inch tube pan sprayed with nonstick cooking spray. Tap the pan once on the kitchen counter to disperse any air bubbles. Bake at 350 degrees for 1 1/4 hours or until a wooden pick inserted in the center comes out clean. Cool in the pan on a wire rack for 10 minutes. Remove the side of the pan and cool for 15 minutes longer. Remove the bottom of the pan and drizzle the warm coffee cake with a mixture of the confectioners' sugar and lemon juice. Let stand until cool.

Petra Mitchell, Watertown

Fat-Free Cinnamon Coffee Cake

PECAN FILLING
1/2 cup packed brown sugar
2 tablespoons all-purpose flour
2 teaspoons ground cinnamon
2 teaspoons vegetable oil
1/2 cup chopped pecans

COFFEE CAKE
1 1/2 cups all-purpose flour
1/2 cup sugar
1 1/2 teaspoons baking powder
1/2 teaspoon salt
3/4 cup skim milk
1/4 cup vegetable oil
1 egg white, lightly beaten

For the filling, mix the brown sugar, flour and cinnamon in a bowl and stir in the oil. Add the pecans and mix well.

For the coffee cake, sift the flour, sugar, baking powder and salt into a bowl and mix well. Add the skim milk, oil and egg white and stir just until moistened. Spoon 1/2 of the batter into an oiled 8×8-inch cake pan and sprinkle with 1/2 of the filling. Top with the remaining batter and sprinkle with the remaining filling. Bake at 375 degrees for 30 minutes or until the coffee cake tests done.

Corky Sharpe, Mt. Juliet

Sour Cream Coffee Cake

NUTTY BROWN SUGAR FILLING
1 cup chopped pecans
1/3 cup packed brown sugar
1 1/2 teaspoons ground cinnamon

COFFEE CAKE
2 cups all-purpose flour
1 teaspoon baking powder
1/2 teaspoon baking soda
1 1/2 cups granulated sugar
3/4 cup (1 1/2 sticks) butter or margarine, softened
1 teaspoon vanilla extract
2 eggs
1 cup sour cream
Confectioners' sugar for dusting

For the filling, mix the pecans, brown sugar and cinnamon in a bowl.

For the coffee cake, mix the flour, baking powder and baking soda in a bowl. Beat the granulated sugar, butter and vanilla in a mixing bowl until light and fluffy. Add the eggs 1 at a time, beating well after each addition. Add the flour mixture and sour cream alternately, beating well after each addition.

Layer the filling and batter 1/2 at a time in a greased 12-cup fluted tube pan or a 10-inch tube pan, beginning with the filling. Bake at 350 degrees for 1 hour or until a wooden pick inserted in the center comes out clean. Cool in the pan on a wire rack for 10 minutes and invert onto the wire rack. Let stand until cool and dust with confectioners' sugar.

Suzanne Walasek, Lebanon

Overnight Coffee Cake

BROWN SUGAR TOPPING
1/4 cup packed light brown sugar
1/4 cup finely chopped pecans
1/4 teaspoon ground cinnamon

COFFEE CAKE
1 cup all-purpose flour
1/2 teaspoon baking powder
1/2 teaspoon ground cinnamon
1/4 teaspoon baking soda
1/2 cup granulated sugar
1/3 cup butter or margarine, softened
1/4 cup packed light brown sugar
1 egg
1/2 cup buttermilk

For the topping, mix the brown sugar, pecans and cinnamon in a bowl.

For the coffee cake, mix the flour, baking powder, cinnamon and baking soda in a bowl. Beat the granulated sugar, butter and brown sugar in a mixing bowl until creamy. Add the egg and beat until blended. Add the flour mixture and buttermilk alternately, beating well after each addition. Spread the batter in a greased 8×8-inch cake pan.

Sprinkle the topping over the batter and chill, covered, for 8 to 10 hours. Remove the cover and bake at 350 degrees for 40 to 45 minutes or until the coffee cake tests done.

Margaret Thompson Kilgore, Lebanon

Yum Yum Coffee Cake

COFFEE CAKE
2 cups all-purpose flour
2 1/4 teaspoons baking powder
2 cups sugar
2 eggs
2 cups undrained crushed pineapple

NUTTY TOPPING
1/4 cup packed light brown sugar
1/4 cup chopped nuts
1/4 teaspoon ground cinnamon

For the coffee cake, sift the flour and baking powder together. Beat the sugar and eggs in a mixing bowl until light and fluffy and stir in the pineapple. Add the flour mixture and mix well. Spread the batter in a greased and floured 9×13-inch cake pan and bake at 350 degrees for 25 to 30 minutes or until the coffee cake tests done.

For the topping, mix the brown sugar, nuts and cinnamon in a bowl and sprinkle over the hot coffee cake.

Charline Smith, Lebanon

Yeast Breads

Basic White Yeast Bread

2 envelopes dry yeast
2 tablespoons sugar
2 cups warm water
6 to 6 1/2 cups all-purpose flour
1/2 cup dry milk powder
2 tablespoons shortening
2 teaspoons salt

Sprinkle the yeast and sugar over the warm water in a bowl. Let stand for 5 minutes or until bubbly. Add 3 cups of the flour, the dry milk powder, shortening and salt and beat for 2 minutes or until blended. Stir in about 3 cups flour to make a soft dough. Knead on a floured surface for 10 minutes or until smooth, adding the remaining 1/2 cup flour if needed to prevent sticking. Shape the dough into a ball and place in a greased bowl, turning to coat the surface. Cover and let rise in a warm place for 1 hour or until doubled in bulk.

Punch the dough down and knead on a floured surface for 1 minute. Divide the dough into 2 equal portions. Cover each portion with a towel and let rest for 10 minutes.

Roll each portion into an 8×12-inch rectangle. Roll as for a jelly roll, beginning at the short sides and sealing the edge and ends. Place seam side down in 2 greased 4×8-inch loaf pans, tucking the ends under. Cover and let rise in a warm place for 1 hour or until doubled in bulk.

Bake at 375 degrees for 30 to 35 minutes or until the loaves sound hollow when tapped. Remove to wire racks to cool.

Ann Sharp, Watertown

Home-Style Yeast Bread

1 envelope dry yeast
2 cups warm water
1 cup sugar
1/2 cup (1 stick) butter or margarine, melted
1 1/2 teaspoons salt
2 eggs, beaten
7 to 8 cups bread flour

Dissolve the yeast in the warm water in a large mixing bowl. Add the sugar, butter, salt, eggs and 4 cups of the flour and beat until smooth. Stir in enough of the remaining flour to form a soft dough. Knead on a lightly floured surface for 6 to 8 minutes or until smooth and elastic. Place in a greased bowl, turning once to grease the top. Cover and let rise in a warm place for 1 hour or until doubled in bulk. Punch the dough down and place on a floured surface. Divide the dough into 3 equal portions. Shape each portion into loaves and place in 3 greased 5×9-inch loaf pans. Cover and let rise for 1 hour or until doubled in bulk. Bake at 350 degrees for 25 to 30 minutes or until golden brown. Invert onto wire racks to cool.

Fay Huddleston, Lebanon

Yeast Loaf Bread

2 envelopes dry yeast
2 cups water
1/3 cup vegetable oil
1 (5-ounce) can evaporated milk
6 to 7 cups all-purpose flour
1 tablespoon salt

Combine the yeast, water, oil and evaporated milk in a microwave-safe container and blend well. Microwave on High until the mixture registers 110 to 115 degrees on a candy thermometer. Add 6 cups of the flour and the salt and mix until smooth. Add enough of the remaining 1 cup flour to form a soft dough. Knead on a lightly floured surface until smooth and elastic. Place in a large bowl greased with shortening, turning to coat. Let rise in a warm place for 45 minutes or until doubled in bulk. Punch the dough down.

Divide the dough into 3 equal portions. Place in 3 greased 5×9-inch loaf pans. Let rise until doubled in bulk. Bake at 350 degrees for 25 to 30 minutes or until golden brown. Invert onto wire racks to cool.

Mary A. Finch, Lebanon

Whole Wheat Bread

2 tablespoons dry yeast
3 cups warm water
8 to 10 cups whole wheat flour or freshly milled wheat
1/4 cup lecithin
2 tablespoons gluten
4 teaspoons salt
2/3 cup vegetable oil
2/3 cup honey
2 eggs

Dissolve the yeast in the warm water in a small bowl. Mix 8 cups of the wheat flour, the lecithin, gluten and salt in a large bowl. Add the yeast mixture, oil, honey and eggs and mix well. Add enough of the remaining 2 cups flour to form a soft dough. Knead on a floured surface until the gluten is fully developed and the dough is smooth and elastic. Cover and let rise until doubled in bulk. Punch the dough down. Divide the dough into equal portions. Shape into loaves and place seam side down into greased 5×9-inch loaf pans. Cover and let rise until doubled in bulk. Bake at 350 degrees for 25 to 30 minutes or until golden brown. Invert onto wire racks to cool.

Joanna Williams, Lebanon

Honey Whole Wheat Bread

$2^1/2$ teaspoons dry yeast
$1^1/4$ cups warm water
1 teaspoon salt
3 tablespoons honey
1 tablespoon wheat bran
1 teaspoon wheat germ
3 tablespoons olive oil
1 cup whole wheat flour
2 cups all-purpose flour
Sesame seeds for sprinkling

Dissolve the yeast in the water in a large bowl. Add the salt, honey, wheat bran, wheat germ, olive oil, whole wheat flour and all-purpose flour and mix to form a soft dough. Place in an oiled bowl, turning to coat the surface. Cover and let rise for 1 hour or until doubled in bulk. Punch the dough down. Knead on a lightly floured surface a few times until smooth and elastic. Cover and let rest for 15 minutes. Shape into a loaf and place seam side down in a greased 5×9-inch loaf pan. Sprinkle with sesame seeds. Cover and let rise in a warm place for 10 to 15 minutes. Bake at 350 degrees for 30 minutes. Invert onto a wire rack to cool.

Petra Mitchell, Watertown

Quick Mix Honeyed Wheat Bread

$5^1/_4$ to $5^3/_4$ cups all-purpose flour
2 cups whole wheat flour
2 envelopes fast-rising yeast
2 teaspoons salt
2 cups milk
1/2 cup water
1/2 cup honey
2 tablespoons vegetable oil

Combine 4 cups of the all-purpose flour, the whole wheat flour, yeast and salt in a large mixing bowl and mix well. Blend the milk, water, honey and oil in a 1 1/2- to 2-quart saucepan. Heat over medium heat until the mixture registers 110 to 115 degrees on a candy thermometer. Add to the flour mixture and mix to blend. Beat at medium speed for 5 minutes or until smooth and elastic. Stir in about 3/4 cup of the remaining all-purpose flour to form a soft dough. Turn the dough onto a board coated with some of the remaining 1/2 to 1 cup all-purpose flour. Knead for 10 minutes or until the dough is smooth and satiny and small bubbles form just under the surface, adding just enough all-purpose flour to prevent the dough from being sticky. Cover the dough and let rest for 10 minutes.

Divide the dough into 2 equal portions. Shape each portion into a loaf and place in 2 greased 4×8-inch loaf pans. Cover lightly with plastic wrap. Let rise in a warm place for 40 to 45 minutes or until doubled in bulk. Bake at 375 degrees for 30 to 45 minutes or until the loaves are brown and sound hollow when tapped. Invert onto wire racks to cool.

Corky Sharpe, Mt. Juliet

Amish Friendship Bread

STARTER

1 cup all-purpose flour
1 cup sugar
1 cup milk
1 cup all-purpose flour
1 cup sugar
1 cup milk
1 cup all-purpose flour
1 cup sugar
1 cup milk

BREAD

Cinnamon-sugar for sprinkling
1 cup starter
1 cup vegetable oil or applesauce
1 cup sugar
1 teaspoon vanilla extract
3 eggs
1/2 cup milk
1 (6-ounce) package vanilla instant pudding mix
2 cups all-purpose flour
1 1/2 teaspoons baking powder
1/2 teaspoon baking soda
1/2 teaspoon salt
2 teaspoons ground cinnamon
1 cup chopped nuts and/or raisins (optional)

For the starter, mix 1 cup flour, 1 cup sugar and 1 cup milk in a bowl. Pour into a large sealable plastic bag and let stand at room temperature for Day 1. On Day 2 through Day 5, squeeze the bag once each day. On Day 6, add 1 cup flour, 1 cup sugar and 1 cup milk to the bag and mix well. On Day 7 through Day 9, squeeze the bag once each day. On Day 10, combine the contents of the bag, 1 cup flour, 1 cup sugar and 1 cup milk in a large bowl and mix well. Pour 1 cup of the starter into each of 4 sealable plastic bags. Keep one for yourself and give the other 3 bags of starter to friends along with instructions for making the bread.

For the bread, grease 2 large loaf pans and sprinkle with cinnamon-sugar. Combine the starter, oil, sugar, vanilla, eggs, milk and pudding mix in a large bowl and mix well. Add the flour, baking powder, baking soda, salt and cinnamon and mix until smooth. Stir in the nuts. Pour into the prepared pans. Bake at 325 degrees for 1 hour or until the loaves test done. Do not use a metal spoon or a metal bowl for mixing. Do not refrigerate. It is normal for the batter to thicken, bubble and ferment.

Scott Hobbs, Lebanon

Sourdough Bread or Rolls

STARTER

3/4 cup sugar
3 tablespoons instant potato flakes
1 cup warm water
1 cup bread flour

3/4 cup sugar
3 tablespoons instant potato flakes
1 cup warm water
1 cup bread flour

BREAD

1/2 cup sugar
1/2 cup corn oil
1 teaspoon salt
1 cup starter
1 1/2 cups warm water
5 cups bread flour
Melted butter for brushing

For the starter, combine 3/4 cup sugar, 3 tablespoons instant potato flakes, 1 cup warm water and 1 cup bread flour in a bowl and mix well. Chill for 5 to 6 days. Remove from the refrigerator and feed by adding 3/4 cup sugar, 3 tablespoons instant potato flakes, 1 cup warm water and 1 cup bread flour; mix well. Cover and let stand at room temperature for 8 to 12 hours. The mixture will bubble, but not rise. Remove 1 cup of the starter to make the bread and return the remaining starter to the refrigerator. Keep refrigerated for 5 to 6 days and then feed again. If you don't make bread, then throw 1 cup of the starter away. The starter must be fed every 5 to 6 days. The starter must be fed 2 or 3 times before giving away.

For the bread, combine the sugar, corn oil, salt, starter, warm water and bread flour in a large bowl and mix well. Place the dough in a greased bowl and turn to coat the surface. Cover lightly with foil and let rise at room temperature for 8 to 12 hours. A warm place will make the dough rise twice as much.

Divide the dough into 3 equal portions. Knead each portion on a floured board a few times. Shape each portion into a loaf and place seam side down in 1 of 3 greased and floured 5×9-inch loaf pans. Brush the tops with melted butter. Cover lightly with foil and let rise for 4 to 12 hours or until doubled in bulk. Bake at 350 degrees on the lowest oven rack for 30 to 35 minutes or until the loaves sound hollow when tapped. Remove from the oven and brush with melted butter. Cool on a wire rack and wrap to store. These bread loaves freeze well.

For rolls, roll out the dough and cut into circles, or pinch off the dough and roll into balls instead of dividing the dough into portions. Place on a greased baking sheet. Continue the directions as above and bake for 15 to 20 minutes or until brown.

Judy Bradshaw, Mt. Juliet

Jan's Sourdough Bread

STARTER

1 recipe starter
1 cup warm water
3/4 cup sugar
3 tablespoons instant potato flakes

BREAD

1 cup starter
1/2 cup vegetable oil
1/4 cup sugar
1 1/2 cups warm water
6 to 7 cups bread flour
Vegetable oil for brushing

For the starter, store starter in the refrigerator loosely covered and feed every 3 to 5 days. Remove the starter from the refrigerator and add the warm water, sugar and instant potato flakes and mix well. Let stand at room temperature for 8 to 10 hours. Remove 1 cup of the starter to make the bread and return the remaining starter to the refrigerator.

For the bread, combine the reserved 1 cup starter, 1/2 cup oil, the sugar, warm water and bread flour in a large bowl and mix to form a stiff dough. Grease the top with vegetable oil or spray with nonstick cooking spray. Cover with waxed paper. Let rise at room temperature for 6 to 7 hours or until doubled in bulk. Punch the dough down. Knead the dough several times on a lightly floured surface. Divide into 3 or 4 equal portions. Knead each portion 8 to 10 times on a floured surface. Shape into loaves and place seam side down in 3 or 4 greased loaf pans. Brush the tops with vegetable oil. Cover with waxed paper and let rise for 6 to 8 hours or until doubled in bulk. Bake at 350 degrees for 25 to 30 minutes or until the loaves test done. Invert immediately onto wire racks to cool.

Jan Fletcher, Lebanon

Sourdough Bread

$1/2$ cup vegetable oil
$1/4$ cup sugar
$1 1/2$ teaspoons salt
$1 1/2$ cups warm water
1 cup starter
6 cups bread flour

Combine the oil, sugar, salt, water, starter and bread flour in a plastic container and mix well. Cover with a damp cloth and let rise for 8 to 12 hours or until doubled in bulk. Punch the dough down. Knead on a lightly floured surface. Shape into loaves and place seam side down in greased 5×9-inch loaf pans. Let rise for 6 hours or until doubled in bulk. Bake at 300 degrees for 30 minutes. Invert onto wire racks to cool.

Mary Lou Ford, Lebanon

Sourdough Whole Wheat Bread

1 cup starter
$1/2$ cup canola oil
$1 1/2$ cups warm water
1 teaspoon salt
5 cups bread flour
1 cup whole wheat flour

Combine the starter, canola oil, water, salt, bread flour and whole wheat flour in a large bowl and mix well. Let rise for 8 hours or until doubled in bulk. Punch the dough down. Knead on a lightly floured surface until smooth and elastic. Divide the dough into 3 equal portions. Shape each portion into a loaf and place in 1 of 3 greased 5×9-inch loaf pans. Let rise for 6 hours or until doubled in bulk. Bake at 350 degrees for 20 to 25 minutes or until golden brown. Invert onto wire racks to cool completely.

Beth Hollingsworth, Mt. Juliet

Herbed Oatmeal Pan Bread

2 cups water
1 cup rolled oats
3 tablespoons butter
3 3/4 to 4 3/4 cups all-purpose flour
1/4 cup sugar
2 teaspoons salt
2 envelopes dry yeast
1 egg
1 tablespoon grated Parmesan cheese
1/2 teaspoon basil
1/4 teaspoon oregano
1/4 teaspoon garlic powder
6 tablespoons butter, melted

Bring the water to a boil in a medium saucepan and stir in the oats. Remove from the heat and stir in 3 tablespoons butter. Cool to 120 to 130 degrees on a candy thermometer.

Combine $1\frac{1}{2}$ cups of the flour, the sugar, salt and yeast in a large mixing bowl and mix well. Add the oats mixture and egg and beat at low speed until moistened. Beat at medium speed for 3 minutes. Stir in $1\frac{3}{4}$ cups to $2\frac{1}{2}$ cups of the flour to form a stiff dough. Knead in the remaining $\frac{1}{2}$ to $\frac{3}{4}$ cup flour on a floured surface for 5 minutes or until smooth and elastic. Shape the dough into a ball and cover with a large bowl. Let rest for 15 minutes. Punch the dough down several times to remove all of the air bubbles and press into a greased 9×13-inch baking pan. Cut diagonal lines $1\frac{1}{2}$ inches apart completely through the dough using a sharp knife. Repeat the cuts in the opposite direction, creating a diamond pattern. Cover loosely with greased plastic wrap and a cloth towel. Let rise in a warm place for 45 minutes or until light and doubled in bulk.

Combine the Parmesan cheese, basil, oregano and garlic powder in a small bowl and mix well.

Uncover the dough and redefine the cuts by inserting the tip of the knife into the cuts until the knife hits the bottom of the pan; do not pull the knife through the dough. Spoon 4 tablespoons of the butter over the cut dough. Bake at 375 degrees for 15 minutes. Brush the remaining 2 tablespoons of the butter over the bread. Sprinkle with the Parmesan cheese mixture. Bake for 10 to 15 minutes or until golden brown.

Charline Shipper Smith, Lebanon

Herb and Garlic Bread

1 envelope dry yeast
1 cup warm water
2 eggs, beaten
2 tablespoons honey
2 teaspoons minced garlic
1 teaspoon basil
1 teaspoon oregano
2 teaspoons salt
2 tablespoons olive oil
3 cups bread flour
Butter for brushing

Dissolve the yeast in the water in a large bowl. Add the eggs, honey, garlic, basil, oregano, salt and olive oil and mix well. Add the flour and mix to form a soft dough. Knead on a floured surface for 10 minutes or until smooth and elastic. Cover and let rise for 10 minutes. Punch the dough down. Shape into a loaf and place seam side down in a 5×9-inch loaf pan. Cover and let rise until doubled in bulk. Bake at 350 degrees for 30 to 45 minutes or until golden brown. Invert onto wire racks and cool for 10 minutes. Brush the top with butter.

René Yarbrough

Challah

1 3/4 cups warm water
2 tablespoons dry yeast
1/2 cup honey
1/4 cup (1/2 stick) butter, melted
1/2 teaspoon salt
1 teaspoon vanilla extract
4 eggs, beaten
7 to 8 cups unbleached flour
1 cup golden raisins
1 tablespoon water
1 teaspoon honey
1 egg yolk
Sesame seeds for sprinkling

Pour the water in a food processor fitted with a steel blade and sprinkle with the yeast. Pulse to dissolve the yeast. Add 1/2 cup honey, the butter, salt, vanilla, eggs and 2 cups of the flour and process to form a sticky dough. Add the raisins and the remaining flour and process until the dough is smooth and elastic. Place the dough in an oiled bowl, turning to coat the surface. Cover and let rise until doubled in bulk. Punch the dough down. Knead a few times until smooth and elastic on a floured surfaced. Cover and let rest for 15 minutes.

Divide the dough into 3 equal portions. Roll each portion into an 18-inch rope. Shape into a braid on an oiled baking sheet and seal the ends. Cover lightly and let rise in a warm place for 45 minutes or until almost doubled in bulk.

Beat the water, 1 teaspoon honey and egg yolk in a bowl until smooth. Brush over the loaf and sprinkle with sesame seeds. Bake at 350 degrees for 45 minutes or until the loaf is brown. Cool on a wire rack.

Petra Mitchell, Watertown

Croissants

$1\frac{1}{2}$ cups (3 sticks) butter or margarine, softened
$\frac{1}{3}$ cup all-purpose flour
2 envelopes dry yeast
$\frac{1}{2}$ cup warm water (110 to 115 degrees)
$\frac{3}{4}$ cup milk
$\frac{1}{4}$ cup sugar
1 teaspoon salt
1 egg
$3\frac{3}{4}$ to $4\frac{1}{4}$ cups all-purpose flour
1 egg yolk
1 tablespoon milk

Cream the butter and $\frac{1}{3}$ cup flour in a mixing bowl. Roll between 2 sheets of waxed paper into a 6×12-inch rectangle. Chill for 1 hour or longer.

Dissolve the yeast in the warm water. Heat $\frac{3}{4}$ cup milk, the sugar and salt in a saucepan, stirring until the sugar dissolves. Remove from the heat and cool to lukewarm. Pour into a large mixing bowl. Add the yeast mixture and egg and beat well. Stir in 2 cups of the flour and beat well. Stir in as much of the remaining flour as possible with a spoon. Knead on a lightly floured surface for 3 to 5 minutes to form a moderately soft dough that is smooth and elastic. Let rest for 10 minutes.

Roll the dough into a 14-inch square. Place the chilled butter mixture on 1/2 of the square. Fold the remaining half of the square over the butter mixture and seal the edges. Roll into a 12×21-inch rectangle and seal the edges. Fold the dough into thirds and roll into a 12×21-inch rectangle. Repeat 2 times, sealing the edges and chilling the dough after each time. Fold the dough into thirds to form a 7×12-inch rectangle. Cover and chill for 3 to 12 hours.

Cut the dough crosswise into quarters. Roll each quarter into a 12-inch circle. Cut each circle into 12 wedges. Roll up each wedge loosely, starting from the opposite side of the point. Place point side down on ungreased baking sheets, curving the ends. Cover and let rise for 30 to 45 minutes or until doubled in bulk.

Beat the egg yolk and 1 tablespoon milk in a small bowl and brush on the rolls. Bake at 375 degrees for 12 to 15 minutes or until golden brown. Remove from the baking sheets to cool.

Petra Mitchell, Watertown

Candy Cane Bread

1 tablespoon dry yeast
1 1/2 cups warm water
1/3 cup vegetable oil
1/3 cup honey
1 egg
4 to 5 cups freshly milled wheat
2 tablespoons lecithin
1 tablespoon gluten
2 teaspoons salt
4 ounces cream cheese, softened
1/2 cup honey
Dried cherries
1 egg
1/4 cup water
1/4 cup honey
Decorating sugar for sprinkling

Dissolve the yeast in 1 1/2 cups warm water in a large bowl. Add the oil, 1/3 cup honey and 1 egg and mix well. Add 4 cups of the wheat, the lecithin, gluten and salt and mix well. Stir in enough remaining 1 cup wheat to form a soft dough. Knead on a floured surface until smooth and elastic and the gluten is fully developed. Cover and let rise until doubled in bulk. Punch the dough down. Shape the dough into a long rope and roll flat. Cut strips along the length of the dough on each side.

Beat the cream cheese and 1/2 cup honey in a mixing bowl until smooth. Spread down the uncut center of the dough. Sprinkle with dried cherries. Fold the side strips of dough alternately over the filling to create a braid. Shape the braid into the shape of a candy cane and place on a baking sheet. Let rise for 30 minutes or until doubled in bulk.

Beat 1 egg, 1/4 cup water and 1/4 cup honey in a bowl until smooth. Bake the braid at 350 degrees for 15 minutes. Remove from the oven and brush with the honey mixture. Sprinkle with decorating sugar. Bake for 5 minutes longer.

Joanna Williams, Lebanon

Egg Braid

2 cups warm water
2 cups all-purpose flour
1 envelope dry yeast
1 cup warm water
1 cup all-purpose flour
1/3 cup sugar
2 eggs, beaten
1/2 cup (1 stick) butter, melted
1 teaspoon salt
4 to 4 1/2 cups all-purpose flour
2 eggs, beaten
Vegetable oil for brushing

Mix 2 cups warm water and 2 cups flour in a crock. Let stand in a warm place for 3 to 4 days or until bubbly and sour. Chill in the refrigerator. Remove the starter from the refrigerator and bring to room temperature before making the bread. Dissolve the yeast in 1 cup warm water. Add 1 cup of the starter and 1 cup flour and mix well. Let stand for 12 to 18 hours to develop a sponge. Stir the sponge to dissolve the crust. Add the sugar, 2 eggs, butter and salt and mix well. Add 2 1/2 cups of the flour and mix well.

Spread 1 cup of the flour on a flat surface. Pour the sponge mixture on the flour. Cover with 1 cup of the flour. Knead until the flour is worked into the dough. Continue adding additional flour if needed to form a stiff dough. Knead the dough 10 times or until folds form. Place in a greased bowl and grease the top. Cover and let rise until doubled in bulk.

Punch the dough down and knead for 2 minutes. Divide the dough into 2 equal portions. Divide 1 portion into 8 equal portions. Roll each of the 8 portions into 12-inch ropes. Place the 8 ropes side by side and braid by folding 1 rope over the other in numerical order. Tuck in the edges. Repeat with the remaining dough. Place the braids on a greased baking sheet. Cover and let rise until doubled in bulk. Brush the braids with the 2 beaten eggs. Bake at 350 degrees for 30 minutes or until golden brown. Remove from the oven and brush with oil. Cool on a wire rack.

Theda Rose, Lebanon

Sourdough Cinnamon Rolls

STARTER

1 envelope dry yeast
1 cup warm water
3 tablespoons instant potato flakes
3/4 cup sugar
3 tablespoons instant potato flakes
3/4 cup sugar
1 cup bread flour
1 cup warm water

ROLLS

1/3 cup sugar
1 tablespoon salt
6 cups bread flour
1 cup starter
1/2 cup vegetable oil
1 1/2 cups warm water
2 tablespoons butter, melted
2/3 cup sugar
2 tablespoons ground cinnamon

For the starter, dissolve the yeast in 1 cup water in a bowl. Stir in 3 tablespoons potato flakes and 3/4 cup sugar. Store in the refrigerator for 5 days. Remove the starter from the refrigerator and feed by adding 3 tablespoons instant potato flakes, 3/4 cup sugar, flour and water. Let stand at room temperature for 8 to 10 hours. Feed the starter twice before making the rolls.

For the rolls, mix 1/3 cup sugar, the salt and bread flour together in a large bowl. Add the starter, oil and water and mix well. Let rise for 8 to 12 hours or until doubled in bulk. Divide the dough into 2 equal portions. Roll each portion into a rectangle and coat with melted butter. Sprinkle each with a mixture of 2/3 cup sugar and the cinnamon. Roll up as for a jelly roll. Cut into 1-inch slices and place in four 9-inch baking pans. Cover and let rise until doubled in bulk. Bake at 350 degrees for 25 to 30 minutes or until golden brown.

Fay Huddleston, Lebanon

Cinnamon Rolls

ROLLS

1 tablespoon dry yeast
$1\frac{1}{2}$ cups warm water
$\frac{1}{3}$ cup vegetable oil
$\frac{1}{3}$ cup honey
1 egg
4 to 5 cups freshly milled wheat
2 tablespoons lecithin
1 tablespoon gluten
2 teaspoons salt
Melted butter for brushing
Cinnamon-sugar to taste

CONFECTIONERS' SUGAR GLAZE

1 cup confectioners' sugar
1 tablespoon milk

For the rolls, dissolve the yeast in the water in a large bowl. Add the oil, honey and egg and mix well. Add the wheat, lecithin, gluten and salt and mix to form a soft dough. Knead on a lightly floured surface until the gluten is fully developed and the dough is smooth and elastic. Cover and let rise until doubled in bulk. Punch the dough down. Shape the dough into a long rope on a lightly floured surface. Roll the rope flat to form a rectangle. Brush with melted butter and sprinkle with cinnamon-sugar to taste. Roll up as for a jelly roll and cut into slices. Place in a baking pan sprayed with nonstick cooking spray. Cover and let rise for 30 minutes or until doubled in bulk. Bake at 350 degrees for 15 minutes.

For the glaze, mix the confectioners' sugar and milk in a bowl until smooth. Drizzle over the hot rolls.

Joanna Williams, Lebanon

Cinnamon Rolls with Glaze

ROLLS

2 eggs, lightly beaten
2 cups milk
1/4 cup (1/2 stick) margarine, melted
3 envelopes fast-rising yeast
6 cups bread flour
1/4 cup sugar
1 tablespoon salt
1/4 cup sugar
2 tablespoons ground cinnamon
1 tablespoon margarine

GLAZE

1 cup confectioners' sugar
1 tablespoon milk

For the rolls, combine the eggs, milk and 1/4 cup margarine in a bowl and mix well. Stir in the yeast. Add the flour, 1/4 cup sugar and salt and stir to form a soft dough. Knead on a floured surface until smooth and elastic. Place in a greased bowl, turning to coat the surface. Cover and let rise until doubled in bulk. Combine 1/4 cup sugar, the cinnamon and 1 tablespoon margarine in a saucepan. Heat until melted, stirring constantly. Punch the dough down. Roll the dough into a rectangle on a lightly floured surface. Brush with the cinnamon mixture and roll up as for a jelly roll. Cut into slices and place in a greased baking pan. Bake at 375 degrees for 20 minutes. Cool on a wire rack.

For the glaze, combine the confectioners' sugar and milk in a bowl and mix well. Spread over the cool rolls.

Mary Preston, Lebanon

Yeast Rolls

2 envelopes dry yeast (1 tablespoon)
2 cups lukewarm water
6 cups all-purpose flour
3/4 cup sugar
1 teaspoon salt
1 cup shortening
Melted butter for brushing

Dissolve the yeast in the water in a small bowl. Mix the flour, sugar and salt in a large bowl. Cut in the shortening until crumbly. Stir in the yeast mixture. Cover and let rise for 8 to 12 hours, punching the dough down several times. Knead on a lightly floured surface until smooth and elastic. Roll into a rectangle on a lightly floured surface and cut into circles. Place side by side on a greased baking sheet and brush with butter. Bake at 350 degrees until brown.

Sarah Jennings, Lebanon

Spoon Rolls

4 cups self-rising flour
$^{1}/_{2}$ cup sugar
1 envelope dry yeast
2 cups warm water
$^{3}/_{4}$ cup ($1^{1}/_{2}$ sticks) margarine, melted
1 egg

Mix the flour and sugar in a bowl. Dissolve the yeast in the water in a large bowl. Add the margarine and egg and mix well. Stir in the flour mixture. Place in an airtight container and seal well. Chill in the refrigerator for 8 to 12 hours or up to 6 days. Spoon the batter into greased muffin cups. Bake at 350 degrees for 20 minutes.

Candy Nation, Lebanon

Index

Wilson County Fair

AWARD-WINNING RECIPES

Wilson County Promotions, Inc.
P.O. Box 1203
Lebanon, Tennessee 37088
615-443-2626
wilsoncountyfair.com

YOUR ORDER	QTY	TOTAL
Wilson County Fair at $15.00 per book		$
Tennessee residents add 9.25% sales tax		$
Postage and handling at $4.00 per book		$
	TOTAL	$

Please make check or money order payable to Wilson County Promotions, Inc.

Name

Street Address

City State Zip

Telephone

Photocopies will be accepted.